A scene from the Broadway production of "The Grapes of Wrath." Set design by Kevin Rigdon.

Photo by Peter Cunningham

JOHN STEINBECK'S
THE GRAPES OF WRATH

BY FRANK GALATI

★

DRAMATISTS
PLAY SERVICE
INC.

The names of FRANK GALATI and JOHN STEINBECK shall be equal in size and on separate lines, no less than 50% of the size, type, color and boldness of the title of the Play in all programs, houseboards, billboards, advertising, posters, circulars, throwaways, announcements of the Play and in all paid publicity under the Producer's control. No names except the title of the Play and the names of the Producer(s) and Star(s) preceding the title shall precede the Authors' names and no names except the title may be larger or more prominent than the Authors' names in size, type, color and boldness.

Anyone receiving permission to produce THE GRAPES OF WRATH is required to give the following acknowledgment on the title page of all programs distributed in connection with performances of the Play:

Originally Produced on the Broadway Stage by The Shubert Organization, Steppenwolf Theatre Company, Suntory International Corporation and Jujamcyn Theatres Corporation.

SPECIAL NOTE ON SONGS AND RECORDINGS

For performances of copyrighted songs, arrangements or recordings mentioned in this Play, the permission of the copyright owner(s) must be obtained (see page 138 for additional information). Other songs, arrangements or recordings may be substituted provided permission from the copyright owner(s) of such songs, arrangements or recordings is obtained; or songs, arrangements or recordings in the public domain may be substituted.

NOTE ON MUSIC

For use of original music by Michael Smith, contact Seminary Music, c/o Michael Peter Smith, 2717 Seminary, Chicago, IL 60614. Telephone: (773) 935-7768.

THE GRAPES OF WRATH was originally produced on the Broadway stage by the Shubert Organization, Steppenwolf Theatre Company, Suntory International Corporation and Jujamcyn Theatres Corporation at the Cort Theatre in New York City on March 22, 1990. It was directed by Frank Galati; the scenery and lighting were by Kevin Rigdon; the costumes were by Erin Quigley; the sound design was by Rob Milburn; original music composed and directed by Michael Smith; dances coordinated by Peter Amster; fight choreography by Michael Sokoloff; the production stage manager was Malcolm Ewen; the stage managers were Janet Friedman and Robyn Karen Taylor; the general manager was Albert Poland; and the general press representative was Fred Nathan. It was presented with the kind permission of Elaine Steinbeck. The cast, in order of appearance, was as follows:

1ST NARRATOR ....Francis Guinan*
JIM CASY ....Terry Kinney*
TOM JOAD ....Gary Sinise*
MULEY GRAVES ....Rick Snyder*
WILLY..Ron Crawford
CAR SALESMEN ....Keith Byron-Kirk, Francis Guinan*,
    Terrance MacNamara, Eric Simonson, Skipp Sudduth
PA ....Robert Breuler*
MA ....Lois Smith
GRANMA ....Lucina Paquet
GRAMPA..Nathan Davis
NOAH ....Jeff Perry*
RUTHIE ....Zoë Taleporos
UNCLE JOHN...James Noah
WINFIELD ....Calvin Lennon Armitage
ROSE OF SHARON...Sally Murphy
CONNIE RIVERS...Mark Deakins
AL ....Jim True*
CAMP PROPRIETOR...............................Terrance MacNamara
THE MAN GOING BACK...................................Francis Guinan*
GAS STATION ATTENDANT.................................Steve Ramsey

GAS STATION OWNER ....Michael Hartman
2ND NARRATOR ....Cheryl Lynn Bruce
AGRICULTURAL OFFICERS ...... Theodore Schulz, P.J. Brown
MAYOR OF HOOVERVILLE.............................Ron Crawford
FLOYD KNOWLES ....Rick Snyder*
CONTRACTOR.....................................Michael Hartman
DEPUTY SHERIFF ....Skipp Sudduth
WEEDPATCH CAMP DIRECTOR ....Francis Guinan*
CAMP NURSE.....................................Nicola Sheara
AL'S GIRL ....Jessica Wilder
ELIZABETH SANDRY............................Cheryl Lynn Bruce
3RD NARRATOR ....Michael Hartman
HOOPER RANCH BOOKKEEPER ....Eric Simonson
HOOPER RANCH GUARD ....Michael Hartman
4TH NARRATOR...............................Skipp Sudduth
MRS. WAINWRIGHT.....................................Rondi Reed*
MR. WAINWRIGHT ....Francis Guinan*
AGGIE WAINWRIGHT ....Kathryn Erbe
THE MAN IN THE BARN ....Lex Monson
HIS SON ....Jeremiah Birkett

* Member of Steppenwolf Theatre Company Ensemble

THE GRAPES OF WRATH was first presented by the Steppenwolf Theatre Company of Chicago (Randall Arney, Artistic
Director; Stephen B. Eich, Managing Director) at the Royal-
George Theatre in Chicago, Illinois in September, 1988 and
was produced in association with AT&T. It was subsequently
produced at the La Jolla Playhouse (Des McAnuff, Artistic
Director; Alan Levey, Managing Director) in La Jolla, California in May, 1989. It was also produced in London, England
at the Royal National Theatre of Great Britain (Thelma Holt,
Executive Producer; Malcolm Taylor, Deputy; Jane Slight, As-
sistant) in June, 1989.

MUSICIANS

GUITAR ....Michael Smith
FIDDLE...Miriam Sturm
HARMONICA, SAW, JAW HARP, BANJO ..................L.J. Slavin
ACCORDIAN, BASS ....William Schwarz

SETTING

Oklahoma and then California, 1938

TABLE OF CONTENTS

AUTHOR'S NOTE

The Steppenwolf ensemble once played this adaptation of
THE GRAPES OF WRATH for an invited audience on a bare
stage in Evanston, Illinois. Though the present text calls for special effects that produce the fundamental natural elements of
earth, fire and water, the play certainly held the stage without
them. The campfires of the migrants, the long trough of water
(covered by a moveable lid on the stage apron) that served as
both the Colorado River and the stream that flooded the boxcar camp and the sheets of rain that drenched the Joads near
the end of the second act in Kevin Rigdon's simple and elo-
quent design for the production were present only in the imagi-
nation of the audience, and yet the grip of the story held tight.

The broken down "truck," the Joad's Hudson Super Six, was
nothing more than a wooden platform on wheels, pushed
around the stage by the actors. But the music, Michael Smith's
haunting score, was still the engine that drove the truck and so
the audience invented the vehicle and saw it move the characters through the story.

This is just to say that THE GRAPES OF WRATH need not
be performed using complex technical effects. Our efforts in de-
signing the play were always to make the most modest use of
available stage craft. We strove to be simple. Simplicity is difficult
to achieve and sometimes the expressive power of stage effects
can overtake story and character. We tried very hard never to let
that happen. In a sense there was no "scenery" in our production: there were natural elements, detailed costumes, and many
real objects. We did feel that the actors needed the "things" that
are precious, necessary for survival and also burdensome to the
characters they played, just as they needed real clothes, not "costumes," to complete the personal environment of each human
being in the story.

Future productions of this play may not have fire and water
and a motorized jalopy, but they may have the power that a
bare stage, a few props and a group of passionate artists can
create.

Frank Galati
Evanston, Illinois
May, 1990

THE GRAPES OF WRATH

ACT I

*An expanse of weathered wood blown over with dust. A frail
barbed-wire fence. Two men, some distance from each other,
on either side of the fence. One, seated on a wooden crate,
plays a rusty wood saw with a violin bow. A simple waltz
melody floats up. The other, looking off into the distance,
listens and lets the melody conclude. His eyes gleam in the
shadow of his broad-brimmed hat.*

FIRST NARRATOR. The dawn came, but no day. *(Particles of
dust hang in the air as feeble light spreads up into the sky.)* In the
morning the dust hung like fog. Men stood by their fences
and looked at the ruined corn, drying fast now, only a little
green showing through the film of dust. And the women came
out of the houses to stand beside their men — to feel whether
this time the men would break. The women studied the men's
faces secretly. For the corn could go, as long as something else
remained. *(Sunlight through a pattern of leaves reveals Jim Casy
sprawled in a pool of dust. He blows into a little harmonica: the
reedy opening notes of "Yes, Sir, That's My Baby."* The man with
the saw and the First Narrator are gone. Casy lowers the harmonica
and picks up the tune in an easy tenor.)*
CASY. *(Singing.)*
    Yes, sir, that's my Saviour
    Jc-sus is my Saviour
    Je-sus is my Saviour now.
    On the level
    'S not the devil,
    Jesus is my Saviour now.
    And by the way...
    And by the way...

* See page 138.

(Tom Joad, in cheap new clothes, walks along the sagging barbed-wire fence. He climbs carefully through, takes off his cap and mops his wet face. A bird whistles nearby.)

TOM. Hi. It's hotter'n hell on the road.

CASY. Now ain't you young Tom Joad — ol' Tom's boy?

TOM. Yeah. All the way. Goin' home now.

CASY. You wouldn't remember me, I guess. Baptized you in the irrigation ditch.

TOM. Why, you're the preacher.

CASY. I was a preacher. Reverend Jim Casy — was a Burning Busher. Used to howl out the name of Jesus to glory. But not no more. Jus' Jim Casy now. Ain't got the call no more. Got a lot of sinful idears — but they seem kinda sensible.

TOM. You're bound to get idears if you go thinkin' about stuff. Sure I remember you. You used to give a good meetin'. I recollect one time you give a whole sermon walkin' on your hands, yellin' your head off. Ma favored you more than anybody. An' Granma says you was just lousy with the spirit. *(Tom digs in his pocket and brings out a pint bottle.)* Have a little snort?

CASY. I ain't preachin' no more much. The sperit ain't in the people much no more; and worse'n that, the sperit ain't in me no more.

TOM. You ain't too damn holy to take a drink are you? *(Tom tosses the bottle to Casy. He drinks.)*

CASY. Nice drinkin' liquor.

TOM. Ought to be. That's fact'ry liquor. Cost a buck. *(Casy takes another swallow.)*

CASY. Yes, sir! Yes, sir! *(Tom moves closer, takes the bottle back and drinks. He squats on his hams.)*

TOM. I ain't seen you in a long time.

CASY. Ain't nobody's seen me. I went off alone, an' I sat and figured. The sperit's strong in me, only it ain't the same. I ain't so sure of a lot of things. *(Casy digs his bony hand into his pocket and brings out a black, bitten plug of tobacco. He brushes it off, bites off a corner and settles the quid into his cheek.)* I used to get the people jumpin' an' talkin' in tongues and glory-shoutin' till they just fell down an' passed out. An' some I'd baptize to bring 'em to. An' then — you know what I'd do?

10

I'd take one of them girls out in the grass, an' I'd lay with her. Done it ever' time. Then I'd feel bad, an' I'd pray an' pray, but it didn't do no good. Come next time, them an' me was full of the sperit, I'd do it again.

TOM. There ain't nothing like a good hot meetin' for pushin' 'em over. I done that myself.

CASY. But you wasn't the preacher. A girl was just a girl to you. But to me they was holy vessels.

TOM. You shoulda got a wife. Preacher an' his wife stayed at our place one time. Jehovites they was. Slep' upstairs. Held meetin's in our barnyard. Us kids would listen. That preacher's missus took a godawful poundin' after ever' night meetin'.

CASY. I'm glad you tol' me. I used to think it was jus' me. Finally it give me such pain I quit an' went off by myself an' give her a damn good thinkin' about.

TOM. You give her a goin' over.

CASY. Well, I was layin' under a tree when I figured her out. Before I knowed it, I was sayin', "The hell with it! There ain't no sin and there ain't no virtue. There's just stuff people do."

TOM. You figured her out.

CASY. I says, "What's this call, this sperit?" An' I says, "It's love. I love people so much I'm fit to bust, sometimes." An' I says, "Don't you love Jesus?" Well, I thought an' thought, an' finally I says, "No, I don't know nobody name' Jesus." I been talkin a hell of a lot. Anyway, I'll tell you one more thing I thought out: an' from a preacher it's the most unreligious thing, and I can't be a preacher no more because I thought it an' I believe it.

TOM. What's that?

CASY. If it hits you wrong, don't take no offense at it, will you?

TOM. I don't take no offense 'cept a bust in the nose. What did you figger?

CASY. I figgered about the Holy Sperit and the Jesus road. I figgered, "Why do we got to hang it all on God or Jesus? Maybe," I figgered, "maybe it's all men an' all women we love; maybe that's the Holy Spirit — the human sperit — the whole shebang. Maybe all men got one big soul ever'body's a part

11

of." Now I sat there thinkin' it, an' all of a sudden — I knew it. I knew it so deep down that it was true, and I still know it.

TOM. You can't hold no church with idears like that. People would drive you out of the country with idears like that. Jumpin' an' yellin'. That's what folks like. Makes 'em feel swell. When Granma got to talkin' in tongues, you couldn't tie her down.

CASY. I baptized you right when I was in the glory rooftree.

TOM. She could knock over a full-growed deacon with her fist.

CASY. Had little hunks of Jesus jumpin' outa my mouth that day.

TOM. Guess I'll mosey along.

CASY. It's a funny thing. I was thinkin' about ol' Tom Joad when you come along. Thinkin' I'd call on him. How is Tom?

TOM. I don't know how he is. I ain't been home in four years.

CASY. Been out travelin' around?

TOM. (Suspiciously.) Didn't you hear about me? I was in the papers.

CASY. No — I never. What?

TOM. I been in McAlester them four years.

CASY. Ain't wantin' to talk about it, huh? I won't ask you no more questions, if you done something bad —

TOM. I'd do what I done — again. I killed a guy. In a fight. We was drunk at a dance. He got a knife in me, an' I killed him with a shovel that was layin' there. Knocked his head plumb to squash.

CASY. You ain't ashamed of nothin' then?

TOM. No, I ain't. I got seven years, account of he had a knife in me. Got out in four — parole. (He shades his eyes.) I hate to hit the sun, but it ain't so bad now.

CASY. I ain't seen ol' Tom in a bug's age.

TOM. Come along.

CASY. I was gonna look in on him anyways. I brang Jesus to your folks for a long time.

TOM. Pa'll be glad to see you. He always said you got too

12

long a pecker for a preacher. *(The two hesitate for a moment and then move off. The sky begins to darken. A man with a guitar crosses the stage. He sings a fragment of a Dust Bowl folk song. Darkness engulfs him and the wind howls. Faint moonlight catches a broken porch column. The column and a few crates define the space that was the Joad house. Tom and Casy emerge in the distance and walk along the fence. A dog barks. Tom sees the fragment of house and stops.)*

TOM. Somepin's happened. They ain't nobody here. *(They climb under the fence and move into the dusty yard.)* Jesus! Hell musta popped here. There ain't nothin' left.

CASY. Le's look in the house. She's all pushed outa shape. Somethin' knocked the hell out of her.

TOM. They're gone — or Ma's dead. If Ma was anywhere's about, that gate'd be shut an' hooked. That's one thing she always done — seen that gate was shut. Ever since the pig got in over to Jacobs' an' 'et the baby.

CASY. If I was still a preacher I'd say the arm of the Lord had struck. But now I don't know what happened. *(Tom lights a match and slips cautiously into the house. He stoops down, finds and lights the stub of a candle, and then picks up a woman's high button shoe.)*

TOM. I remember this. This was Ma's. It's all wore out now. Ma liked them shoes. Had 'em for years. No — they're gone — or dead. *(Muley Graves suddenly appears in the shadows.)*

MULEY. Tommy?

TOM. Muley!

MULEY. When'd you get out, Tommy?

TOM. Two days ago. Took a little time to hitchhike home. An' look here what I find. Where's my folks, Muley?

MULEY. They're all at your Uncle John's. The whole brood. Gettin' money together so they can shove on west. Uncle John got *his* notice too.

TOM. You know this here preacher, don't you Muley? Rev. Casy.

MULEY. Why, sure, sure. Didn't look over. Remember him well.

TOM. What happened here?

MULEY. Well, your folks was gonna stick her out when the

13

bank come to tractorin' off the place. Bumped the hell outa the house, an' give her a shake like a dog shakes a rat.

CASY. Why they kickin' folks off the lan'?

MULEY. Bank can't afford to keep no tenants. Them sons-a-bitches. Them dirty sons-a-bitches. I tell ya, men, I'm stayin'. They ain't gettin' rid a me.

TOM. Sure. I wonder Pa went so easy. I wonder Grampa didn' kill nobody. *(Casy begins gathering splinters of wood and dry twigs. He builds and lights a fire.)* Nobody never tol' Grampa where to put his feet. An' Ma ain't nobody you can push aroun' neither. I seen her beat the hell out of a tin peddler with a live chicken one time 'cause he give her a argument. She had the chicken in one han', an' the ax in the other, about to cut its head off. She aimed to go for that peddler with the ax, but she forgot which hand was which, an' she takes after him with the chicken. Couldn't even eat that chicken when she got done. They wasn't nothin' but a pair a legs in her han'. *(Casy puts a match into the pile of twigs.)* Grampa throwed a hip outa joint laughin'. *(The fire lights.)* How'd my folks go so easy?

MULEY. T'wernt easy, Tommy. Took somepin' outa your Pa. Kinda got to 'im.

CASY. Fella gets use' to a place, it's hard to go.

MULEY. Well, sir, it's a funny thing. Somepin' went an' happen to me when they tol' me I had to get off the place. Fust I was gonna go in an' kill a whole flock a people. But there wasn't nobody you could lay for. Who's the Shawnee Lan' and Cattle Company? It ain't nobody. It's a company. Got a fella crazy. Then all my folks all went away out west. An' I got wanderin' aroun'. I'm jus' wanderin' aroun' like a damn ol' graveyard ghos'. I been goin' aroun' the places where stuff happened. Like there's a... *(The three men move close around the fire.)* ...a place down by the barn where Pa got gored to death by a bull. An' his blood is right in that groun', right now. Mus' be. Nobody never washed it out. An' I put my han' on that groun' where my own pa's blood is part of it. *(He swallows.)* You fellas think I'm touched?

CASY. No. You're lonely — but you ain't touched.

TOM. If your folks went to the west, you should have went too. You shouldn't have broke up the fambly.

MULEY. I couldn'. Somepin just wouldn' let me. I — I ain't talked to nobody for a long time.

CASY. You should talk. Sometimes a sad man can talk the sadness right out through his mouth. *(The sound of a car pulling up and stopping in the distance. A dog barks. Casy puts out the fire.)*

TOM. What the?...

MULEY. That's prob'ly the supe'ntendent of this stretch a cotton. Somebody maybe seen our fire.

TOM. We ain't done no harm. *(Muley and Casy rush into the house.)*

MULEY. Get down. We're trespassin'. We can't stay.

TOM. We'll jus' set here. We ain't doin' nothin'.

CASY. Git in here, Tom. You're on parole. *(Casy blows out the candle. Tom follows them into the house.)*

MULEY. They been tryin' to catch me for two months. Now duck.

TOM. Won't they come in here with a flashlight an' look aroun' for us? I wisht I had a stick.

MULEY. Na, they won't. Willy done that one night an' I clipped 'im from behind with a fence stake. Knocked him colder'n a wedge. *(Willy appears in the distance with a flashlight.)*

WILLY. Muley? Muley?

MULEY. He got somebody with 'im tonight.

WILLY. Ain't here. *(Willy moves off. Tom stands suddenly. His eyes blaze.)*

TOM. I never thought I'd be hidin' out on my old man's place. *(Tom, Casy and Muley are engulfed in darkness. A guitar sounds and light reveals five car salesmen leering over their bow-ties.)*

1ST SALESMAN. Used cars.

2ND SALESMAN. Good used cars.

3RD SALESMAN. Cheap transportation.

4TH SALESMAN. Used cars.

ALL FIVE SALESMEN. *(Singing.)*
    Cadillacs, LaSalles, Buicks,
    Plymouths, Packards, Chevies,

Fords, Pontiacs. Soften 'em up, Joe.

Jesus. I wisht I had a thousand jalopies!

Get 'em ready to deal, an' I'll close 'em.

Goin' to California? Here's just what you need.

(A rusted heap of truck rolls over the expanse of dust and wood. The front is a Hudson Super Six sedan, its top cut off in the middle and a truck bed fitted on.)

She looks shot, but they's thousan's of miles in her.

Get 'em ready to deal, an' I'll close 'em.

1ST SALESMAN. *(Speaking.)*

There's a dumb-bunny lookin' at the Graham.

See if he got any jack in his jeans.

2ND SALESMAN. *(Speaking.)*

Some a these farm boys is sneaky.

1ST SALESMAN. *(Speaking.)*

Soften 'em up an' roll 'em in to me Joe.

You're doin' good.

ALL FIVE SALESMEN. *(Singing.)*

Steer him by that busted Hudson

Tell him ain't no finer in Salisaw.

She can do fifty. Easy.

I bet you, boy, if Moses had drove her

He'd a rested his head in California.

(They whistle "California, Here I Come"* and slip away. As the afternoon light creeps over the dust, the area around the truck is revealed, littered with piled furniture, crates and most of the Joad family's belongings. Uncle John's house is in the background, a weathered wooden wall with an old screen door. Pa stands in the truck bed nailing on the top rails of the truck sides. His grizzled face is low over his work. He sets a nail and his hammer thunders it in. Tom emerges. Casy hangs back in the distance.)

TOM. Pa.

PA. What do you want? *(His hammer is suspended in the air. He turns and looks at Tom. The hammer drops slowly to his side.)* It's Tommy. It's Tommy come home. Tommy. You ain't busted out? You ain't got to hide?

* See page 138.

TOM. Naw. I'm paroled. I'm free. I got my papers. *(Pa lays his hammer down and drops gently to the ground.)*
PA. Tommy. We are goin' to California. But we was gonna write you a letter an' tell you. But you're back. You can go with us. You can go! *(There is a crash inside the house.)*
MA'S VOICE. Ruthie, cut that out.
PA. Your ma got a bad feelin' she ain't never gonna see you no more. Almost she don't want to go to California, fear she'll never see you no more. *(Another crash.)* Le's surprise 'em. Le's go in like you never been away. Le's jus' see what your ma says. *(Pa grabs his son by the shoulders. He sees Casy.)*
TOM. You remember the preacher, Pa. He come along with me.
PA. He been in prison too?
TOM. No, I met him on the road. He's been away. *(Pa and Casy shake hands.)*
PA. You're welcome here, sir.
CASY. Glad to be here. It's a thing to see when a boy comes home. It's a thing to see.
PA. Home.
CASY. To his folks. *(Ma Joad emerges through the screen door with a bucket.)*
MA. Pa, run out to the barn now an' git Granma and Grampa.
PA. Ma, there's a couple fellas jus' come along the road, an' they wonder if we could spare a bite.
MA. Let 'em come. We got a' plenty. Tell 'em they got to wash their han's. I'm jus' takin' up the sidemeat now. Lucky I made plenty a bread this aft... *(She sees Tom, puts the bucket down and moves toward him soundlessly in her bare feet. Her face is full of wonder.)* Thank God. Oh, thank God! *(She stops.)* Tommy, you ain't wanted? You didn't bust loose?
TOM. No, Ma. Parole. I got the papers... *(He pats his breast pocket.)* here. *(Her small hand feels his arm, and then her fingers graze his cheek. Tom pulls his under lip between his teeth and bites.)*
MA. I was scared we was goin' away without you — and we'd never see each other again.

17

PA. Fooled ya, huh, Ma? We aimed to fool ya, an' we done it. Jus' stood there like a hammered sheep. Wisht Grampa'd been here to see it. Grampa woulda whacked 'imself so hard he'd a throwed his hip out.

TOM. Where is Grampa? I ain't seen the ol' devil.

MA. Oh, him an' Granma are havin' their nap, they sleeps in the barn. Pa, run out an' tell 'em Tommy's home. Grampa's a favorite of him.

PA. A course. I should of did it before. *(Pa crosses the yard, swinging his hands high.)*

MA. Tommy.

TOM. Yeah?

MA. Tommy, I got to ask you — you ain't mad?

TOM. Mad, Ma?

MA. You ain't poisoned mad? You don't hate nobody? They didn't do nothin' in that jail to rot you out with crazy mad?

TOM. No-o-o. I was for a little while. But I ain't proud like some fellas. I let stuff run off'n me.

MA. Thank God!

TOM. Ma, when I seen what they done to our house...

MA. Tommy, don't you go fightin' 'em alone. They'll hunt you down like a cayote. They say there's a hun'red thousand of us shoved out. If we was all mad the same way, Tommy, they wouldn't hunt nobody down.

TOM. Many folks feel that way?

MA. I don't know. They're jus' kinda stunned. Walk aroun' like they was half asleep.

GRANMA'S VOICE. Oh Lord! Pu-raise Gawd fur vittory! *(Tom turns his head and grins.)*

TOM. Granma finally heard I'm home. *(Ma turns away.)* Ma, you never was like this before! *(Her face hardens and her eyes grow cold.)*

MA. I never had my house pushed over. I never had my fambly stuck out on the road. I never had to sell — ever'thing.

GRANMA'S VOICE. Hallelujah!

MA. Here they come now. *(From across the yard come Grampa, buttoning his fly, Granma, hobbling in her hiked up Mother Hubbard, and Pa. Ma returns to the little house.)*

GRAMPA. Where is he?

GRANMA. Pu-raise Gawd fur vittory!

GRAMPA. (*Fumbles with his buttons.*) Goddamnit, where is he? (*He stops.*) Lookit him. A jailbird. Ain't been no Joads in jail for a hell of a time. Got no right to put 'im in jail. He done just what I'd do. Sons-a-bitches got no right. An' some stinkin' skunk, braggin' how he'll shoot ya when ya come out. I sent word to 'im, I says "You lay your sights anywhere near Tommy an' I'll take it an' I'll ram it up your ass," I says. Scairt 'im, too. (*Grampa slaps Tom on the chest.*)

GRANMA. Pu-raise Gawd fur vittory! (*Ma comes from the house with steaming tin plates of sidemeats and biscuits. She takes them to the dusty old table near the truck. Twelve-year-old Ruthie and ten-year-old Winfield stand in the doorway. Uncle John emerges from around the back of the house.*)

TOM. How ya keepin' yaself, Grampa?

GRAMPA. I always said Tom would come bustin' outa that jail like a bull through a corral fence. An' you done it!

TOM. I didn't bust out. They lemme out.

GRAMPA. Get outa my way. I'm hungry.

TOM. Ain't he a heller? (*Granma approaches Tom vaguely. Grampa sits and gulps biscuits. Ruthie and Winfield come out of the house and sit on the ground.*)

GRANMA. (*Embracing Tom.*) A wicketer, cussin'er man never lived. He's goin' to hell on a poker, praise Gawd! Wants to drive the truck! Well he ain't goin' ta. (*Noah, tall and strange, with a calm but puzzled look on his face, wanders in carrying farm tools.*)

TOM. How ya, Noah?

NOAH. Fine. How a you? (*He walks off slowly behind the truck. Pa shakes his head.*)

TOM. Uncle John?

UNCLE JOHN. Glad to see ya, Tommy. (*They shake hands. Tom meets the children near Uncle John.*)

TOM. Hello, how you kids?

WINFIELD. Hello.

RUTHIE. All right. (*Ma comes from the house with more steaming plates.*)

MA. Jus' get yourself a plate an' set down wherever you can. Here's Rosasharn and Connie come just in time for supper. *(Rose of Sharon and her nineteen year-old husband Connie Rivers approach from the distance. She walks with a light grace; her hair, braided and wrapped around her head, makes an ash-blond crown that glows in the sunset light. Connie carries a carpet bag.)*

PA. Rosasharn's been nestin' with Connie's folks. By God! You don't even know Rosasharn's married to Connie Rivers — Rosasharn's due too 'bout three-four-five months now. Swellin' up right now.

MA. Rosasharn look here's Tommy. He's paroled! *(Ma returns to the house.)*

TOM. Jesus! Rosasharn was just a little kid. *(Rose of Sharon pulls Connie up to Tom.)*

ROSE OF SHARON. This is Connie, my husband. *(The two men look each other over and then shake hands. Tom moves to Rose of Sharon.)*

TOM. Well, I see you been busy.

ROSE OF SHARON. You do not see, not yet. *(Everyone laughs.)*

TOM. Pa jus' now tol' me. When's it gonna be?

ROSE OF SHARON. Oh, not for a long time!

TOM. Gonna get 'im bor in a orange ranch, huh?

ROSE OF SHARON. You do not see. *(Ma comes from the house with two pots full of food.)*

MA. Rosasharn git over here and hep me git this food on the table. *(Rose of Sharon moves to Ma, takes the pots to the table and serves the rest of the food.)*

TOM. Hey! Where's the preacher? He was right here. Where'd he go?

GRANMA. Preacher? You got a preacher? Go git him we'll have a grace. *(She points to Grampa.)* Too late for him — he's et. Go git the preacher. *(Casy emerges from behind the truck.)*

TOM. Jim Casy! What was you doin', hidin'?

CASY. Well, no. But a fella shouldn't butt his head in where a fambly got fambly stuff. I was just settin' a-thinkin'.

TOM. Come on an' eat. Granma wants a grace.

CASY. But I ain't a preacher no more.

TOM. Aw, come on. Give her a grace.

MA. *(To Casy.)* You're welcome.

PA. You're welcome. Have some supper.

GRANMA. Grace fust. Grace fust.

GRAMPA. Oh, that preacher. Oh, he's all right. I always liked him since I seen him — *(He winks lecherously.)*

GRANMA. Shut up, you sinful ol' goat.

CASY. I got to tell you, I ain't a preacher no more.

GRANMA. Say her.

CASY. If me jus' bein' glad to be here an' bein' thankful for people that's kind and generous, if that's enough — why, I'll say that kinda grace.

GRANMA. Say her. An' get in a word about us goin' to California. *(Casy bows his head. The family members ranged around the dusty yard, seated and standing, holding battered tin plates of meat and bread, bow their heads in turn. Casy's eyes search the sky in silence.)*

CASY. I been thinkin'. I been in the hills thinkin', almost you might say like Jesus went into the wilderness to think His way out of a mess of troubles.

GRANMA. Pu-raise Gawd!

CASY. I ain't sayin' I'm like Jesus. But I got tired like Him, an' I got mixed up like Him, an' I went into the wilderness like Him, without no campin' stuff.

GRANMA. Hallelujah!

CASY. An' I got thinkin', on'y it wasn't thinkin', it was deeper down than thinkin'. I got thinkin' how there was the moon an' the stars an' the hills, an' there was me lookin' at 'em, an' we wasn't separate no more. We was one thing. An' that one thing was holy.

GRANMA. Oh, yes. Pu-raise Gawd! Hallelujah!

CASY. I got thinkin' how we was holy when we was one thing, an' mankin' was holy when it was one thing. An' it on'y got unholy when one mis'able little fella got the bit in his teeth an' run off his own way, kickin' and draggin' an fightin'. Fella like that bust the holiness. But when they're all workin' together — kind of harnessed to the whole shebang — that's right, that's holy. An' then I got thinkin' I don't even know

21

what I mean by holy. I can't say no grace like I use' ta say. I'm glad of the holiness of supper. I'm glad there's love here. That's all. *(Heads remain bowed. Casy looks around.)* I've got your supper cold. Amen.

ALL. A-men. *(Ma withdraws into the house. Casy moves and sits on a chair away from the table. Pa and Tom move away from the table with their dinner plates. Grampa trails after them.)*

PA. Your brother Al looked this Hudson over 'fore we bought her. He says she's all right.

TOM. What's he know? He's just a squirt.

PA. He worked for a company. Drove truck last year. He knows quite a little. Smart aleck like he is. He knows. He can tinker an engine, Al can.

TOM. Where's he now?

PA. *(Under his breath, leaning close to Tom.)* Well, he's a-billy goatin' aroun'. Tom-cattin' hisself to death. Smart-aleck sixteen-year-older, an' his nuts is just a-eggin' him on. *(Turning to the others.)* A plain smart aleck. Ain't been in nights for a week.

GRAMPA. I was worse. I was much worse. I was a heller, you might say.

TOM. You look like a heller yet, Grampa.

GRAMPA. Well, I am, kinda. But I ain't nowhere's near the fella I was. Jus' let me get out to California where I can pick me an orange when I want it. Or grapes. There's a thing I ain't never had enough of.

PA. If I ain't mistaken, there's a young smart aleck draggin' his tail home right now ... Looks purty wore out, too. *(Al Joad comes into the yard and moves to the table with a swagger. When he recognizes Tom, his boasting face changes, admiration and veneration shine in his eyes.)*

TOM. Hello, Al. Jesus, you're growin' like a bean! I wouldn't of knowed you. *(He sticks out his hand, and Al's hand jerks out to meet it.)* They tell me you're a good hand with a truck.

AL. I don't know nothin' much about it.

PA. Been smart-aleckin' aroun' the country. You look wore out.

AL. Did — did you bust out? Of jail?

TOM. No. I got paroled.

AL. (*Disappointed.*) Oh. (*Al moves away from Tom and goes to the table to eat. Tom moves over and sits on the ground near Casy. Grampa reaches into his half-buttoned fly and contentedly scratches under his testicles. Ma comes out of the house.*)

MA. Here. (*Moves to Grampa.*) Let me button you up. (*Grampa struggles but Ma holds him and buttons his underwear and his fly.*)

GRAMPA. (*Sputters angrily.*) I want to be let to button my own pants.

MA. (*Playfully.*) They don't let people run aroun' with their clothes unbutton in California.

GRAMPA. They don't, hey! Well, I'll show 'em. I'll go aroun' a-hangin' out if I wanta! (*Granma shakes her head and goes into the house.*)

MA. Seems like his language gets worse ever' year. Showin' off, I guess.

GRAMPA. Know what I'm a-gonna do when I get out there? I'm gonna pick me a whole bunch of grapes offa bush or whatever and squash 'em on my face an' let the juice run offen my chin. An' I'm gonna fill me a whole wash tub full a grapes, an' I'm gonna set in 'em, an' scrooge aroun', an' let the juice run down my pants. (*Noah laughs.*)

TOM. When ya thinkin' a startin' Pa?

PA. (*Nodding at Al.*) Well now that this one's back from his squirtin' aroun' I figger maybe we could start tomorrow or day after. Quicker we get started, surer it is we get there. Fella says it's damn near two thousan' miles.

MA. Ruthie'n Winfield pick up the plates. Rosasharn bring out my washtub.

ROSE OF SHARON. I got to be careful, Ma. I cain't lif'!

CONNIE. I'll get her.

UNCLE JOHN. Al, help me with this over here. (*Al, Noah and Uncle John move behind the truck. Pa climbs on the back bed and squats down, while Grampa moves and sits in a chair by the house. Ruthie and Winfield pick up the plates and then go into the house. Rose of Sharon follows Connie into the house to get the washtub. Casy moves far off watching the sun hang like a drop of blood over the broken earth. Ma moves to Tom and sits on a chair.*)

MA. Tom, I hope things is all right in California.

TOM. What makes you think they ain't?

MA. Well — nothing. Seems too nice, kinda. I seen the han' bills fellas pass out, an' how much work they is, an' high wages an' all; an' I seen in the paper how they want folks to come an' pick grapes an' oranges an' peaches. That'd be nice work, Tom, pickin' peaches. I'm scared of stuff so nice. I ain't got faith.

TOM. Don't roust your faith bird-high an' you won't do no crawlin' with the worms.

MA. I know that's right. That's Scripture ain't it?

TOM. I guess so. Sure sounds like it. *(Connie brings a wash-tub from the house and places it near Ma. Rose of Sharon lights a lantern and hangs it on the house near the door. Casy sits on the running board of the truck and plays "Amazing Grace" on the har-monica.)*

MA. Still ... I like to think how nice it's gonna be, maybe, in California. Never cold. An' fruit ever' place, an' people just bein' in the nicest places, little white houses in among the orange trees. I wonder — that is, if we all get jobs an' all work — maybe we can get one of them little white houses.

TOM. Maybe. *(Suddenly Pa stands up in the back of the truck.)*

PA. I got me an idear! What we hangin' aroun' for? I want to get shut of this. Now we're goin', why don't we go? *(Uncle John emerges from behind the truck followed by Noah and Al.)*

UNCLE JOHN. We could get ready by daylight and go.

NOAH. All we gotta do is get that pork salted.

PA. They say it's two thousan' miles.

AL. That's a hell of a long ways.

TOM. We oughta go.

PA. Noah, you cut up the meat and the rest of us'll start loadin' the truck.

MA. How about if we forgit somepin'? Not seein' it in the dark?

NOAH. We could look around after daylight. *(Ruthie and Winfield explode out of the house and climb up in the front seat of the truck.)*

PA. We got to get the stuff together. Come on you fellas. *(Casy steps out of the shadows.)*

CASY. I — I wonder if I kin go along with you folks. Somepin's happening. I went over an' I looked, an' the houses is all empty an' the lan' is empty, an' this whole country is empty. I can't stay here no more. I — I got to go where the folks is goin'. *(Pa and Uncle John look at each other. The Joad men gather together, and Casy moves away.)*

PA. We got to figger close. It's a sad thing to figger close. Le's see, now. There's Grampa an' Granma — that's two. An' me an' John an' Ma — that's five. An' Noah an' Tommy an' Al — that's eight. Rosasharn an' Connie is ten, an' Ruthie an' Winfiel' is twelve.

NOAH. An' two cut-up pigs.

PA. Kin we feed a extra mouth? Kin we Ma?

MA. *(Firmly.)* It ain't kin we! It's will we? As far as "kin," we can't do nothin', not go to California or nothin'; but as far as "will," why we'll do what we will. An' as far as "will" — it's a long time our folks been here and east before, an' I never heerd tell of no Joads or no Hazletts, neither, ever refusin' food an' shelter or a lift on the road to anybody that asked. They's been mean Joads, but never that mean.

PA. But s'pose there just ain't room? S'pose we jus' can't all get in the truck?

MA. There ain't room now. There ain't room for more'n six, an' twelve is goin' sure. One more ain't gonna hurt. *(Casy emerges from behind the truck.)*

PA. Well, Reverend, as long as you're goin' with us, git over here an' give me a han'! *(The man with the guitar and three other musicians appear near the truck and let rip a bright galloping tune.)* Ma, clear off the table, Noah's got to cut up that meat. Got salt?

MA. Yes. Got plenty salt. Got two nice kegs. *(Suddenly the family begins to function. Noah brings slabs of meat from the house. Pa hammers quickly at the truck, and Casy lights a lantern. Circles of lantern light move about in the yard. The men bring together all the things to be taken and begin piling them near the truck. Tom collects tools. Ma lays bricks of meat in a keg and covers each layer with salt. The music urges all of this on.)*

TOM. Ma what stuff we gonna take from the kitchen? *(Rose*

25

of Sharon brings out armloads of clothes and begins folding them and packing them into a wooden box. She gets into the box and tramps them down with her bare feet as she packs.)

MA. The bucket. All the stuff to eat with: plates an' cups, the spoons an' knives an' forks. Put all in a drawer, an' take the drawer. *(Tom returns to the house.)* The big fry pan an' the big stew kettle, the coffee pot. Take the rack outa the oven. That's good over a fire. I'd like to take the wash tub, but I guess there ain't room. I'll wash clothes in the bucket. *(Tom carries a drawer out of the house.)* Don't do no good to take little stuff. You can cook little stuff in a big kettle, but you can't cook big stuff in a little pot. *(Casy approaches Ma, indicating that he'll salt the pork. Ma goes into the house. Al and Pa are at the truck.)*

AL. *(Lifting a lantern.)* Pa, I just had a thought.

PA. Yeah?

AL. Tom is parole! That means he can't go outside the state. If they catch him, they send 'im back for three years.

PA. Jesus Christ, I hope that ain't true. We need Tom.

AL. Right.

PA. Al ... where you been the las' two weeks?

AL. Stuff a fella got to do when he's leavin' the country.

PA. Don't tell your Ma 'bout Tom. *(The music swells up. Al and Pa get back to work. Tom lights a small fire and crouches by it, fanning the flames. Rose of Sharon brings Tom his old jacket; he goes into the house to change. Ma comes out of the house with an old metal box and moves to the fire. Ma sits near the fire and opens the box. The music changes. The guitar gently plays the simple waltz melody. Faint light begins to appear. Ma removes some postcards and papers from the box and looks them over. Putting them back in the box, she takes out a pair of gold earrings and holds them up to her ears for a moment. She puts them in her pocket, closes the box, stands and with resignation tosses the box on the fire. The waltz melody ends.)*

MA. Guess we oughta wake up Granma and Grampa. Gettin' along towards day.

AL. Here comes Grampa. They's somepin' wrong with 'im. *(Grampa has come from the barn. His eyes are dull and cold. Dawn*

26

light spreads over the yard.)

GRAMPA. Ain't nothin' the matter with me. I jus' ain't a-goin'.

PA. Not goin'? What you mean? We got to go. We got no place to stay. *(Granma appears from behind the truck.)*

GRAMPA. I ain't sayin' for you to stay. You go right along. Me — I'm stayin'. I give her a goin'-over all night mos'ly. This here's my country. I b'long here. An' I don't give a goddamn if they's oranges an' grapes crowdin' a fella outa bed even. I ain't a-goin'.

MA. Why Grampa, you ain't slep all night! Now you let your boys set you down on a nice mattress we got fixed up here. *(She signals to the men.)* I got some soothin' sirrup make you nice and drowsy and after you nap a little we'll have a long talk about you stayin' right here where you belong. *(Ma rises and moves over to the men with the bottle of syrup. The men hoist Grampa into the truck.)*

GRAMPA. I ain't a-goin'. I ain't a-goin'.

GRANMA. What's all this? What you doin' now, so early? *(Al moves around the fully loaded truck inspecting it.)*

AL. Chr-ist, looks like we got the whole farm on 'er. *(To Pa.)* If it rains we'll tie the tarp to the bar above, an' the folks can get underneath, out of the wet. Up front we'll be dry enough.

PA. That's a good idear. You done real good.

TOM. Jesus Christ, it's near sunrise. We got to get goin'. Come on.

PA. Al, start 'er up. *(Al turns on the ignition. The little band of musicians starts up a rhythm which spatters and then dies. All the Joads stop dead and turn to look at the truck. Al restarts the engine. The music turns the engine over and it begins to hum and run in easy rhythm. When the way is clear, the truck backs up to center and pivots to face front. Ma crosses over to the fire and looks at her chair, which she decides to leave. The yard is now clear of all the Joads belongings except the truck and the chair.)* Ma, you an Rosasharn set in with Al for a while. We'll change aroun' so it's easier, but you start out that way. *(Ma and Rose of Sharon get into the front seat with Al. Tom puts out the small fire and brings Ma's chair to the truck. Connie, Granma, Ruthie and Winfield pile up on top of the load. Pa, Uncle John and Casy climb on. Noah looks underneath the truck.)*

NOAH.   Holy Jesus, them springs is flat as hell.

AL.   Lucky I blocked up under 'em. *(Noah climbs up. When everyone is settled, Tom hops up on the running board, and the music begins to travel.)* Ain't you gonna look back, Ma? *(She shakes her head.)*

MA.   We're goin' to California, ain't we? Awright then, let's go to California.

AL.   Chr-ist, whata load! We ain't makin' no time on this trip. *(Muley emerges in the distance and watches the Joads leave. The Band members dig their heels into the arid soil and sing bitterly. The weathered wall of Uncle John's house very slowly lifts up out of sight behind the truck.)*

MAN WITH GUITAR.   *(Singing.)*
>Sixty-Six is the path of a people in flight
>Refugees from dust and shrinking land
>From the thunder of tractors
>From the twisting winds
>That howl up out of Texas
>From the floods
>And the twisting winds

(The truck pivots to the right and begins slowly to move.)

BAND.   *(Singing.)*
>From all of these
>The people are in flight
>They come into Sixty-Six
>From the tributary side roads
>From the wagon tracks
>From the rutted country roads
>Sixty-Six is the mother road
>The mad flight

(The band moves away leaving only the fiddle player. A mournful gospel tune drifts from the fiddle. The truck stops and the Joads unload. The men emerge carrying Grampa's body wrapped in an old quilt. They place it on the ground in the distance. Connie climbs down and lights a campfire near the back of the truck. Rose of Sharon puts a crude tripod with a kettle hanging from it over the fire. Casy lights

*two lanterns, and then he and Connie open a grave-sized trap. Ruthie
sits near the fire peeling potatoes. Winfield moves solemnly away, collects a couple of twigs, sits down, and begins tying them together with
a bit of string, fashioning a cross. The men gather, leaning on shovels and mattocks. Granma is laying in the back of the truck. Ma
comes from behind the truck with a lantern.)*
GRANMA. Will! Will!
MA. Rosasharn...
GRANMA. Will!
MA. ...like a good girl go lay down with Granma. She needs
somebody now. She's knowin', now. *(Rose of Sharon climbs up
into the back of the truck. Ma goes to the corpse.)*
PA. We got to figger what to do. They's laws. You got to re-
port a death, an' when you do that, they either take forty dollars for the undertaker or they take him for a pauper.
UNCLE JOHN. We never did have no paupers.
TOM. Maybe we got to learn. We never got booted off no
land before, neither. *(Ma tears a strip from her apron and ties up
the dead man's jaw. The men stir restively near the fire as Ma moves
dreamily over the corpse.)*
PA. Grampa buried his pa with his own hand, done it in dig-
nity, an' shaped the grave nice with his own shovel. That was
a time when a man had the right to be buried by his own son
an' a son had the right to bury his own father.
UNCLE JOHN. The law says different now.
PA. Sometimes the law can't be foller'd no way. Not in decency, anyways. They's lots a times you can't. Sometimes a fella
got to sift the law. I'm sayin' now I got the right to bury my
own pa. Anybody got somepin' to say?
CASY. Law changes, but "got to's" go on. You got the right
to do what you got to do.
PA. *(Turns to Uncle John.)* It's your right too, John. You got
any word against?
UNCLE JOHN. No word against. On'y it's like hidin' him
in the night. Grampa's way was t'come out a-shootin'.
PA. We can't do like Grampa done. We got to get to California 'fore our money gives out.
TOM. Sometimes fellas workin' dig up a man an' they raise

hell an' figger he been killed. The gov'ment's got more inter-
est in a dead man than a live one. They'll go hell-scrapin'
tryin' to fin' out who he was and how he died. I offer we put
a note of writin' in a bottle an' lay it with Grampa, tellin' who
he is an' how he died, an' why he's buried here.

PA. That's good. Wrote out in a nice han'. Be not so lonesome too, knowin' his name is there with 'im, not jus' a old
fella lonesome underground. Any more stuff to say? Tom, you
get over there now and get that paper wrote. Uncle John,
Noah, Al; let's get started. You too, Connie. *(The men move up
to the grave and begin to dig. They pile the dark soil on the lid of
the open trap, working in relays with two shovels. Rose of Sharon
climbs out of the truck. Ruthie moves to join Winfield.)*

MA. *(Moves to Rose of Sharon.)* How's Granma?

ROSE OF SHARON. Sleepin'. *(Tom approaches.)*

TOM. We got any paper an' pen, Ma?

MA. *(Shakes her head slowly.)* No-o. That's one thing we didn'
bring. *(Casy digs in his pocket. Ma moves around the fire to the cab
of the truck.)*

CASY. Here's a pencil. *(Casy hands a small stubby pencil to Tom
then moves over to the truck, picks up two lanterns, and joins the men
digging.)*

MA. *(Draws an old book out of the truck.)* Here's the Bible.
They's a clear page in front. Use that an' tear it out. *(Ma
hands Tom the Bible. He sits down in the firelight and squints his
eyes in concentration. As he begins slowly to write, Rose of Sharon
pulls Ma away from the fire.)*

ROSE OF SHARON. Ma, I got to ask.

MA. Scared again? Why, you can't get through nine months
without sorrow.

ROSE OF SHARON. But will it — hurt the baby?

MA. They used to be a sayin', "A chile born outa sorrow'll
be a happy chile."

ROSE OF SHARON. But it might hurt anyway.

MA. 'F you go greasin' yourself an' feelin' sorry, an' tuckin'
yourself in a swalla's nest, it might. Forget that baby for a
minute. He'll take care of hisself.

CASY. *(To Pa.)* Let me at that a while would ya? *(Pa stops dig-*

ging and gives his shovel to Casy. Ma pulls a fruit jar out of a box on the side of the truck and begins wiping it out. Rose of Sharon sits down and peels potatoes.)

TOM. Ma, listen to this here. "This here is William James Joad, dyed of a stroke, old old man. His fokes buried him becaws they got no money to pay for funerls. Nobody kilt him. Jus a stroke and he dyed." (Ma moves down and sits next to Tom.)

MA. Why, that soun's nice. Can't you stick on somepin from Scripture so it'll be religious? Open up an' git a sayin', somepin outa Scripture.

TOM. Got to be short. I ain't got much room lef' on the page.

MA. How 'bout "God have mercy on his soul?"

TOM. No, sounds too much like he was hung. I'll copy somepin'. (He turns the page and reads. The men are nearing the end of the digging.)

PA. Good an' deep. A couple feet more.

TOM. Here's a good short one. "An' Lot said unto them, Oh, not so, my Lord."

MA. Don't mean nothin'. Long's you're gonna put one down, it might's well mean somepin. Turn to Psalms, over futher. You kin always get somepin outa Psalms. (Pa, Uncle John, Al and Connie move to the corpse. Noah and Casy continue digging.)

NOAH. Funny thing is — losin' Grampa ain't made me feel no different than I done before. I ain't no sadder than I was.

CASY. It's just the same thing. Grampa an' the old place, they was just the same thing.

NOAH. He was gonna squeeze grapes over his head, an' all stuff like that.

CASY. He was foolin', all the time. I think he knowed it. An' Grampa didn' die tonight. He died the minute we took 'im off the place.

TOM. Now here is one. This here's a nice one, just blowed full a religion. (The four men carry Grampa's body and lower it gently into the grave. Tom reads.) "Blessed is he whose transgression is forgiven, whose sin is covered." How's that? (Ma is standing above Tom.)

MA. That's real nice. (She hands him the jar.) Put that one in.

And turn the lid nice and tight. *(Pa calls over to Ma.)*

PA. How about Granma?

MA. Sleepin'. Maybe she'd hold it against me, but I ain't a-gonna wake her up. She's tar'd. *(Tom places the page in the jar and screws the lid down tight.)*

PA. We oughta have a prayer. Will ya he'p us?

CASY. I'll he'p you folks, but I won't fool ya. *(The family, all but Granma, begins to gather around the grave. Winfield gives the cross to Tom, who puts it and the jar in with Grampa. Connie moves to Rose of Sharon.)*

PA. *(To Casy.)* Ain't none of our folks ever been buried without a few words.

CASY. I'll say 'em. *(Connie pulls Rose of Sharon along.)*

CONNIE. You got to. It ain't decent not to. It'll just be a little.

CASY. It'll be a short one. *(He bows his head. The others follow. Connie leads Rose of Sharon closer to the group.)* This here ol' man jus' lived a life an' jus' died out of it. I don't know whether he was good or bad, but that don't matter much. He was alive, an' that's what matters. Heard a fella tell a poem one time, an' he says, "All that lives is holy." Got to thinkin', an' purty soon it means more than the words says. An' I wouldn't pray for a ol' fella that's dead. He's awright. He got a job to do, but it's all laid for 'im an' they's on'y one way to do it. But us, we got a job to do, an' they's a thousan' ways, an ' we don' know which one to take. An' if I was to pray, it'd be for the folks that don' know which way to turn. Grampa here, he got the easy straight. An' now cover 'im up and let 'im get to his work. Amen.

ALL. Amen. *(A strand of gospel music soars up on a distant fiddle. The men shovel the dirt back into the grave. Connie puts out the fire and helps pack up the camp. The man with the guitar emerges and joins the melody of the fiddle. When the men slam the grave-trap shut, the music abruptly changes. Tom and the family climb on the truck and the rest of the band emerges and joins the man with the guitar. They sing a Dust Bowl hymn. The truck backs up slowly and pivots front. The guitar churns the melody along. Al cocks his head as he drives. Ma and a sleeping Winfield are in the front seat.)*

AL. Makes a racket, but I think she's awright. God knows what she'll do if wc got to climb a hill with the load we got. Got any hills 'tween here an' California, Ma?

MA. Seems to me they's hills. 'Course I dunno. But seems to me I heard they's hills an' even mountains. Big ones.

AL. We'll burn right up if we got climbin' to do. Have to throw out some a' this stuff. Maybe we shouldn' a brang that preacher.

MA. You'll be glad a that preacher 'fore we're through. That preacher'll help us.

AL. Ma — Ma, you scared a goin'? You scared a goin' to a new place?

MA. A little. Only it ain't like scared so much. I'm jus' a settin' here waitin'. When somepin happens that I got to do somepin — I'll do it.

AL. Ain't you thinkin' what's it gonna be like when we get there? Ain't you scared it won't be nice like we thought?

MA. No. No, I ain't. You can't do that. I can't do that. It's too much livin' too many lives. Up ahead they's a thousan' lives we might live, but when it comes, it'll on'y be one. If I go ahead on all of 'em, it's too much. You got to live ahead 'cause you're so young, but — it's jus' the road goin' by for me. An' it's jus' how soon they gonna wanta eat some more pork bones. That's all I can do. I can't do no more. All the rest'd get upset if I done any more'n that. They all depen' on me jus' thinkin' about that. *(Al turns the steering wheel; the truck pivots and moves off. Groups of people emerge and begin to set up camp, pitch tents and build fires. People in the camps gather around the man with the guitar and sing a Dust Bowl road song. Groups of men gather. Their faces are strong and muscled under the harsh light. Some sit, some stand. The proprietor, a sullen lanky man, sits in a chair and drums his fingers on his knee. Pa, Uncle John, Connie and Noah are among the men. Al, Tom and Casy approach them from the distance. The proprietor drops his front chair legs to the floor and leans forward.)*

PROPRIETOR. *(To Tom.)* You men wanta camp here?

TOM. No. We got folks here. We dropped 'em off. Hi, Pa.

PA. Thought you was gonna be all week. Get her fixed?

TOM. We was pig lucky. Got a part 'fore dark. We can get goin' furst thing in the mornin'.

PA. That's a pretty nice thing. Ma's worried. Ya Granma's off her chump.

PROPRIETOR. If you three fellas wanta camp here it'll cost you four bits. Get a place to camp an' water an' wood. An' nobody won't bother you.

TOM. What the hell. We can sleep in the ditch right beside the road, an' it won't cost nothin'. *(The proprietor drums his knee with his fingers.)*

PROPRIETOR. Deputy sheriff comes on by in the night. Might make it tough for ya. Got a law against sleepin' out in this state. Got a law against vagrants.

TOM. If I pay you a half a dollar I ain't a vagrant, huh?

PROPRIETOR. That's right. *(Tom's eyes glow angrily.)*

TOM. Deputy sheriff ain't your brother-in-law by any chance?

PROPRIETOR. *(Leaning forward.)* No, he ain't. An' the time ain't come yet when us local folks got to take no talk from you goddamn bums, neither.

TOM. It don't trouble you none to take our four bits. An' when'd we get to be bums? We ain't asked ya for nothin'. All of us bums, huh? Well, we ain't askin' no nickels from you for the chance to lay down an' rest. *(The men are rigid, motionless, quiet. Expressions are gone from their faces. Their eyes, in the shadows under their hats, move secretly to the face of the proprietor.)*

PA. Come off it, Tom.

TOM. Sure, I'll come off it. I don't wanta make no trouble. It's a hard thing to be named a bum. I ain't afraid. I'll go for you an' your deputy with my mitts — here now, or jump Jesus. But there ain't no good in it.

PROPRIETOR. Ain't you got half a buck?

TOM. Yeah, I got it. But I'm gonna need it. I can't set it out jus' for sleepin'.

PROPRIETOR. Well, we all got to make a livin'.

TOM. Yeah, on'y I wisht they was some way to make her 'thout takin' her away from somebody else.

PA. We'll get movin' smart early. Look, mister. We paid. These here fellas is part a our folks. Can't they stay? We paid a dollar and a half.

PROPRIETOR. For nine. Three more is another fifty cents.

TOM. We'll go along the road. Come for ya in the morning. *(To the proprietor.)* That awright with you?

PROPRIETOR. If the same number stays that come an' paid — that's awright.

TOM. We'll go along pretty soon. *(Pa speaks generally. The men shift their positions.)*

PA. It's dirt hard for folks to tear up an' go. Folks like us that had our place. We ain't shif'less. 'Till we got tractored off, we was people with a farm. *(A young thin man turns his head slowly.)*

YOUNG MAN. Croppin'?

PA. Sure we was sharecroppin'. Used' ta own the place.

YOUNG MAN. Same as us.

PA. Lucky for us it ain't gonna las' long. We'll get out west an' we'll get work an' we'll get a piece of growin' land with water. *(A man in a ragged coat, huddled in a corner, laughs and then moves out of the shadows.)*

MAN GOING BACK. You folks must have a nice little pot a money.

PA. No, we ain't got no money. But they's plenty of us to work, an' we're all good men. Get good wages out there an' we'll put 'em together. We'll make out. *(The Man Going Back laughs again. His laughter turns hysterical, a high whining giggle, then dissolves into a fit of coughing.)*

MAN GOING BACK. You goin' out there — oh, Christ. You goin' out an' get — good wages — oh, Christ! Pickin' oranges maybe? Gonna pick peaches?

TOM. We gonna take what they got. They got lots a stuff to work in. *(The Man Going Back giggles under his breath.)* What's so goddamn funny about that?

MAN GOING BACK. You folks all goin' to California, I bet.

PA. I tol' you that. You didn' guess nothin'.

MAN GOING BACK. Me — I'm comin' back. I been there. I'm goin' back to starve. I'd ruther starve all over at once.

PA. What the hell you talkin' about? I got a han'bill says they got good wages, an' little while ago I seen a thing in the pa-

35

per says they need folks to pick fruit.

MAN GOING BACK. I don' wanna fret you.

TOM. You ain't gonna fret us. You done some jackassin'. You ain't gonna shut up now. The han'bill says they need men.

MAN GOING BACK. You don't know what kind a men they need.

TOM. What you talkin' about?

MAN GOING BACK. Look. How many men they say they want on your han'bill?

PA. Eight hunderd, an' that's in one little place.

MAN GOING BACK. Orange color han'bill?

PA. Why — yes.

MAN GOING BACK. Give the name a the fella — says so and so, labor contractor? *(Pa reaches in his pocket and brings out a folded orange handbill.)*

PA. That's right. How'd you know?

MAN GOING BACK. Look. It don't make no sense. This fella wants eight hunderd men. So he prints up five thousand of them things an' maybe twenty thousan' people sees 'em. An' maybe two-three thousan' folks get movin' account a this here han'bill. Folks that's crazy with worry.

PA. But it don't make no sense!

MAN GOING BACK. Not till you see the fella that put out this here bill. You'll see him, or somebody that's working for him. You'll be a-campin' by a ditch, you an' fifty other families. An' he'll look in your tent an' see if you got anything lef' to eat. An' if you got nothin', he says, "Wanna job?" An' you'll say, "I sure do, mister. I'll sure thank you for a chance to do some work." An' he'll say, "I can use you." An' you'll say, "When do I start?" An' he'll tell you where to go, an' what time, an' then he'll go on. Maybe he needs two hunderd men, so he talks to five hunderd, an' they tell other folks an' when you get to the place, they's a thousan' men. This here fella says, "I'm payin' twenty cents an hour." An' maybe half the men walk off. But they's still five hunderd that's so goddamn hungry they'll work for nothin' but biscuits.

PROPRIETOR. You sure you ain't one of these here troublemakers? You sure you ain't a labor faker?

36

MAN GOING BACK. I swear to God I ain't!
PROPRIETOR. They's plenty of 'em. Goin' aroun' stirrin' up
trouble. Gettin' folks mad. Chiselin' in. They's plenty of 'em.
Time's gonna come when we string 'em all up, all them troublemakers. We gonna run 'em outa the country. Man wants to
work, OK. If he don't — the hell with him. We ain't gonna
let him stir up no trouble.
MAN GOING BACK. I tried to tell you folks. Somepin it
took me a year to find out. Took two kids dead, took my wife
dead to show me. But I can't tell you. I should of knew that.
Nobody couldn't tell me, neither. I can't tell ya about them
little fellas layin' in the tent with their bellies puffed out an'
jus' skin on their bones, an' shiverin' an' whinin' like pups,
an' me runnin' aroun' tryin' to get work — not for money,
not for wages! Jesus Christ, jus' for a cup of flour an' a spoon
a lard. An' then the coroner come. "Them children died a
heart failure," he said. Put it on his paper. Shiverin', they was,
an' their bellies stuck out like a pig bladder. (*He looks around
at the men, their mouths open a little, breathing shallowly, then turns
and walks away into the darkness. A car zooms by on the highway.
The men are silent and uneasy. Finally one speaks.*)
MAN. Gettin' late. Got to sleep.
PROPRIETOR. Prob'ly shif'less. They's so goddamn many
shif'less fellas on the road now. (*Ma steps out of the shadows to
meet the Joad men.*)
MA. All sleepin'. Granma finally dozed off.
PA. Fella was jus' sayin' —
TOM. Funny what he says. Says they's lots a folks on the way.
MA. I'm just a-twitterin' to go on. Wanta get where it's rich
and green. Wanta get there quick.
PA. Ever'body settled in?
MA. All but Connie an' Rosasharn. They went off to sleep in
the open. Says it's too warm in camp. (*Pa turns to Tom and
Casy. Ma folds her arms and walks away.*)
PA. S'pose he's tellin' the truth — that fella?
CASY. He's tellin' the truth awright. The truth for him. He
wasn't makin' nothin' up.
TOM. How about us? Is that the truth for us?

CASY. I don' know.

PA. I don' know. (*The guitar begins to churn. Swiftly the people strike their little tents and move away. The truck backs on and the Joads climb aboard as the truck moves, and turns forward. The litany of the road is chanted over the driving engine of the guitar.*)

MAN WITH GUITAR. Clarksville, Ozark, Van Buren and Fort Smith on Sixty-Four, and there's an end of Arkansas. And all the roads into Oklahoma City, Sixty-Six down from Tulsa, Two-Seventy up from McAlester, Eighty-One from Wichita Falls south, from Enid north. Edmond, McLoud, Purcell, Sixty-Six out of Oklahoma City; El Reno and Clinton, going west on Sixty-Six. Hydro, Elk City, and Texola; and there's an end to Oklahoma. Sixty-Six across the Panhandle of Texas. Shamrock and McLean, Conway and Amarillo, the yellow. Wildorado and Vega and Boise, and there's an end to Texas. (*Several others join the singing. A gas station sign appears, and the gas attendant and the station owner move to the truck.*)

SINGERS. Tucumcari and Santa Rosa and into the New Mexican mountains to Albuquerque, where the road comes down from Santa Fe. Then down the gorged Rio Grande to Los Lunas and west on Sixty-Six again to Gallup, and there's the border of New Mexico. (*The gas station attendant carries a large can of water. Al moves out of the truck and opens the hood. Tom moves to the owner.*)

ATTENDANT. You people sure have got nerve.

TOM. What you mean?

ATTENDANT. Well, startin' out in a jalopy like this.

TOM. It don't take no nerve to do somepin when there ain't nothin' else you can do. Well, thanks. We'll drag on. (*Tom pays the station owner and climbs back in the driver's seat of the truck. Al slams the hood and hops in. The owner and the attendant move away from the truck. The band plays travelling music. The attendant shakes his head and speaks.*)

ATTENDANT. Jesus, what a hard-looking outfit!

OWNER. Them Okies? They're all hard-lookin'.

ATTENDANT. Jesus, I'd hate to start out in a jalopy like that.

OWNER. Well, you and me got sense. Them goddamn Okies got no sense and no feeling. They ain't human. A human being wouldn't live like they do. A human being couldn't stand to be so dirty and miserable. They ain't a hell of a lot better than gorillas.

ATTENDANT. Just the same I'm glad I ain't crossing the country in no Hudson Super-Six. She sounds like a threshing machine.

OWNER. You know, they don't have much trouble. They're so goddamn dumb they don't know it's dangerous. And, Christ Almighty, they don't know any better than what they got. Why worry?

ATTENDANT. I'm not worrying. Just thought if it was me, I wouldn't like it.

OWNER. That's 'cause you know better. They don't know any better. *(They wander off shaking their heads. The man with the guitar churns the engine of the truck again. A woman steps into the light.)*

SECOND NARRATOR. Holbrook, Joseph City, Winslow. They drove all night and came to the mountains in the night. They passed the summit in the dark and came slowly down in the late night... *(The guitar flares. A fiddle joins in. The sky begins to lighten again. A long dark trough of water is revealed.)* And when the daylight came they saw the Colorado River below them. The Joads drove to the river and sat looking at the lovely water flowing by, and the green reeds jerking slowly in the current. *(She kneels and begins to scrub a shirt in the water. Tom leans out of the truck. Ruthie and Winfield hop off the truck, and run down to the river and sit. They dangle their feet in the dark water.)*

TOM. Mind if we stop here a piece?

SECOND NARRATOR. We don't own it, mister. Stop if you want. They'll be a cop down to look you over. *(Tom turns the truck around. The second narrator rings out the shirt and moves away. The truck is now parked with its curtained rear end facing forward just above the trough of dark water.)*

TOM. We got the desert. We got to get water and rest. *(Ma calls to the children from the truck.)*

MA. Ruthie! Winfiel'! You come back. *(Pa climbs out of the truck and signals to the children.)*

PA. Come on, you kids. *(They climb out of the water and run off with Pa. Ma and Rose of Sharon climb out of the back of the truck. Rose of Sharon brings a bucket down to the water. Connie stretches out lazily by the water away from Ma and Rose of Sharon. Tom, Noah, and Al move above the truck and work on the engine. Uncle John and Casy drift off in different directions.)*

ROSE OF SHARON. Ma ... Ma, when we get there, you all gonna pick fruit an' kinda live in the country, ain't you?

MA. We ain't there yet. We don't know what it's like. We got to see.

ROSE OF SHARON. Me an' Connie don't want to live in the country no more. We got it all planned up what we gonna do.

MA. Ain't you gonna stay with us — with the family?

ROSE OF SHARON. Well, we talked about it, me an' Connie. Ma, we wanna live in a town. Connie gonna get a job in a store or maybe a fact'ry. An' he's gonna study at home, maybe radios, so he can get to be a expert an' maybe later have his own store. An' we'll go to pitchers whenever. An' Connie says I'm gonna have a *doctor* when the baby's born; an' he says we'll see how times is, an' maybe I'll go to a hospiddle. An' we'll have a car, little car. An' when he gets done studying at night, why — it'll be nice, an' he tore a page outa *Western Love Stories*, an' he's gonna send off for a course... *(Al has crawled out from under the truck and is listening.)* 'cause it don't cost nothin' to send off. Says right on that clipping. I seen it. An' we'll live in town an' go to pitchers whenever, an' — well. *I'm* gonna have a *'lectric iron!* An', well, I thought maybe we could all go in town, an' when Connie gets his store — maybe Al could work for him.

MA. We don' want you to go 'way from us. It ain't good for folks to break up. *(Al glowers at Rose of Sharon.)*

AL. Me work for Connie? How about Connie comes a-workin' for me? He thinks he's the on'y son-of-a-bitch can study at night? *(He stomps off as Rose of Sharon storms to the truck and climbs in the back. Connie follows Al a few steps, and then moves above the truck. Casy appears and moves to the riverbank. Ma car-*

ries the full bucket back to the truck and climbs in. Rose of Sharon closes the faded curtain at the rear of the truck. Tom appears in his long underwear and moves around the truck down to the water. Tom is grimy from working on the truck. He and Casy sit at the riverbank.)

TOM. You been awful goddamn quiet the past few days. Whatsa matter — gettin' sour?

CASY. I done enough talkin' when I was a preacher to las' me the resta my life.

TOM. Yeah, but you done some talkin' sence, too.

CASY. I'm all worried up. I been watchin' the cars on the road, them we passed an' them that passed us. I been keepin' track.

TOM. Track a what?

CASY. They's hundreds a families like us all a-goin' west. They ain't none of 'em goin' east. Did you notice that?

TOM. Yeah I noticed.

CASY. It's like a whole country movin'.

TOM. Well, they is a whole country movin'! We're movin' too.

CASY. Well s'pose all these here folks an' everybody, s'pose they *can't* get no jobs out there?

TOM. Goddamn it! How'd I know? I'm jus' puttin' one foot in fronta' the other. I done it at Mac for four years, jus' marchin' in cell an' out cell an' in mess an' out mess. Jesus Christ, I thought it'd be different when I come out!

CASY. Now look, Tom...

TOM. I'm gonna take a bath ... I'm gonna wash an' I'm gonna sleep in the shade all day long.

CASY. Oh, what the hell! So goddamn hard to say anything. *(Casy walks away as Tom slips into the river. Al runs on, strips, and jumps into the water. Noah wanders on.)*

AL. Jesus, I needed this. *(Noah follows and jumps into the river in his overalls. They sit holding themselves with heels dug into the river bottom. Pa strolls down, and sits on the bank. Tom begins washing himself. Pa looks up into the distance.)*

PA. We come through them?

TOM. Got the desert yet. An' I hear she's a son-of-a-bitch.

NOAH. Gonna try her tonight?

41

TOM. What ya think, Pa?

PA. Well, I don't know. Do us good to get a little res', 'specially Granma. But other ways, I'd kinda like to get acrost her an' get settled into a job.

NOAH. Like to jus' stay here. Like to lay here forever. Never get hungry and never get sad. Lay in the water all life long, lazy as a brood sow in the mud.

TOM. Never seen such tough mountains. This here's a murder country. This here's the bones of a country. Wonder if we'll ever get in a place where folks can live 'thout fightin' hard scrabble an' rocks. I seen pitchers of a country flat an' green, an' with little houses like Ma says, white. Ma got her heart set on a white house. Get to thinkin' they ain't no such country.

PA. Wait till we get to California. You'll see nice country then.

AL. *(To Noah.)* Better scrunch down under water. She'll burn the livin' Jesus outa you. *(He dunks Noah under water. They fight and splash. Al leaps out of the water, grabs his clothes and runs off. Pa hoists himself up and moves away. Noah's wide eyes scan the mountain range in the distance.)*

NOAH. Tom!

TOM. Yeah?

NOAH. Tom, I ain't a-goin' on.

TOM. What you mean?

NOAH. Tom, I ain't a-gonna leave this here water. I'm a-gonna walk on down this here river.

TOM. You're crazy.

NOAH. Get myself a piece of line. I'll catch fish. Fella can't starve beside a nice river.

TOM. How 'bout the fam'ly? How 'bout Ma?

NOAH. I can't he'p it. I can't leave this here water. You know how it is, Tom. You know how the folks are nice to me. But they don't really care for me.

TOM. You're crazy.

NOAH. No, I ain't. I know how I am. I know they're sorry. But — Well, I ain't a-goin'. You tell Ma — Tom.

TOM. Now you look-a-here...

NOAH. No. I'm a-gonna go now, Tom — down the river.

I'll catch fish an' stuff, but I can't leave her. I can't. You tell Ma, Tom. *(Noah climbs out of the water, scoops up his clothes and starts off.)*
TOM. Listen, you goddamn fool —
NOAH. It ain't no use. I'm sad, but I can't he'p it. I got to go. *(Noah runs off up the river. Tom climbs out of the water and gathers his clothes. He looks after Noah, then moves slowly off. Ma opens the curtain at the back of the truck. Granma's head is at the back. She is resting under a faded pink curtain. Ma wrings out a cloth over the bucket and rests it on Granma's head. Rose of Sharon climbs down with the bucket.)*
GRANMA. Will! Will! You come here, now. I tol' him to come right here. I'll catch him. I'll take the hair off'n him. *(Ma climbs down with an old piece of cardboard; she sits on the back of the truck and begins to fan Grandma.)*
ROSE OF SHARON. She's awful sick. *(Rose of Sharon puts down the bucket and sits on the step at the back of the truck, resting her head on her mother's knee.)*
MA. When you're young, Rosasharn, ever'thing that happens is a thing all by itself. It's a lonely thing, I know, I 'member Rosasharn. You're gonna have a baby, Rosasharn, and that's somepin to you lonely and away. That's gonna hurt you, and the hurt'll be a lonely hurt, an' this here truck is alone in the worl'. They's a time of change, an' when that comes, dyin' is a piece of all dyin', and bearin' is a piece of all bearin', an' bearin' an' dyin' is two pieces of the same thing. An' then things ain't lonely any more. An' then a hurt don't hurt so bad, 'cause it ain't a lonely hurt no more, Rosasharn. I wisht I could tell you so you'd know, but I can't. Take an' fan Granma. That's a good thing to do. I wisht I could tell you so you'd know. *(Ma climbs down and hands the cardboard to Rose of Sharon, she hops up next to Granma and begins to fan her. Ma picks up the bucket as Pa appears and approaches her.)*
GRANMA. Will! You dirty! You ain't never gonna get clean. *(Tom, now dressed, approaches the truck. Casy appears some distance away, then Connie and finally Al and Uncle John.)*
TOM. Ma, I got somepin' to tell ya. Noah — he went on down the river. He ain't a-goin' on.

MA. Why?

PA. Ain't goin'? What the hell is the matter with him?

TOM. I don't know. Says he got to. Says he got to stay. Says for me to tell you.

MA. How'll he eat?

TOM. I don' know. Says he'll catch fish.

MA. Family's fallin' apart. I don' know.

PA. My fault. That boy is all my fault!

TOM. He'll be awright, Ma. He's a funny kind a fella.

MA. I jus' can't seem to think no more.

PA. My fault.

TOM. No.

PA. I don't want to talk about it no more. I can't — my fault. *(Pa moves around to the front of the truck. He gives one of the fenders a violent kick. Ma looks at Uncle John, and then turns to Tom. Al climbs into the driver's seat. The guitar plays an old hymn. The truck pivots very slowly and faces front. Ma moves down to the river, pours Granma's bath water out of the bucket, then moves up and gets into the truck. Al moves over as Tom gets in the driver's seat. The music changes and begins again to travel. The truck is suspended in a glow of light, and the fiddle cries far off. The headlights snap on, casting two yellow beams ahead. Al and Tom peer into the dark from the cab. Rose of Sharon and Connie sit on the load above the cab. They kiss deeply. Rose of Sharon pulls away.)*

AL. So this here's the desert! Jesus, what a place. How'd you like to walk acrost her?

TOM. People done it. Lots a people done it; an' if they could, we could.

AL. Lots must a died.

TOM. Well, we ain't come out exactly clean. *(Desert stars are hung in the soft night sky and the truck turns. Uncle John and Casy sit high-up on the side of the truck.)*

UNCLE JOHN. Casy, you're a fella oughta know what to do.

CASY. What to do about what?

UNCLE JOHN. I dunno.

CASY. Well, that's gonna make it easy for me!

UNCLE JOHN. Well, you been a preacher.

CASY. Look, John, ever'body takes a crack at me 'cause I been a preacher. A preacher ain't nothin' but a man.

UNCLE JOHN. Yeah, but — he's a *kind* of a man, else he wouldn' be a preacher. I wanna ast you — well, you think a fella could bring bad luck to folks?

CASY. I dunno. I dunno.

UNCLE JOHN. Well — see — I was married — fine, good girl. An' one night she got a pain in her stomach. An' she says, "You better get a doctoi." An' I says, "Hell you jus' et too much." She give me a *look.* An' she groaned all night, an' she died the next afternoon. You see, I kil't her. An' sence then I tried to make it up — mos'ly to kids. An' I tried to be good, an' I can't. I get drunk, an' I go wild.

CASY. Ever'body goes wild. I do too.

UNCLE JOHN. Yeah, but you ain't got a sin on your soul like me.

CASY. Sure I got sins. Ever'body got sins. A sin is somepin you ain't sure about. Them people that's sure about ever'thing an' ain't got no sin — well, with that kind a son-of-a-bitch, if I was God I'd kick their ass right outa heaven! I couldn' stand 'em!

UNCLE JOHN. I got a feelin' I'm bringin' bad luck to my own folks.

CASY. A man got to do what he got to do.

UNCLE JOHN. You think it was a sin to let my wife die like that?

CASY. Well, for anybody else it was a mistake, but if you think it was a sin — then it's a sin. A fella builds his own sins right up from the groun'.

UNCLE JOHN. I got to give that a goin'-over. *(The truck turns again, its rear facing front. A flashlight beam flicks over the load, and the shadowy figures of two officers become visible as Tom cuts off the engine. Tom and Pa climb out of the truck.)*

TOM. What's this here? *(The second officer copies down the number from the rear license plate.)*

1ST AGRICULTURAL OFFICER. Agricultural inspection. We got to look over your stuff. Got any vegetables or seeds?

TOM. No.

45

1ST AGRICULTURAL OFFICER. Well, we got to look over your stuff. You got to unload. *(Ma partly opens the curtain at the back of the truck.)*

MA. Look, mister. We got a sick ol' lady. We got to get her to a doctor. We can't wait. You can't make us wait.

2ND AGRICULTURAL OFFICER. Yeah? Well, we got to look you over. *(Ma seems to be fighting with hysteria.)*

MA. I swear we ain't got any thing! I swear it. An' Granma's awful sick. *(Ma opens the curtain further. She cradles Granma in her arms.)* Look. *(The officer shines his light on Granma's face.)*

2ND AGRICULTURAL OFFICER. By God, she is. Go on ahead. *(Ma drops the curtain. Pa gets in the cab of the truck next to Al. Tom climbs back in the driver's seat and starts the motor. The officers walk away.)* I couldn' hold 'em.

1ST AGRICULTURAL OFFICER. Maybe it was a bluff.

2ND AGRICULTURAL OFFICER. Oh, Jesus, no! You should of seen that ol' woman's face. That wasn't no bluff. *(The officers move off into the dark. The truck turns and faces front. The guitar and fiddle race over the wind. The First Narrator is alone in light. The beams of the headlights burn dimly.)*

FIRST NARRATOR. All night they bored through the hot darkness, and jackrabbits scuttled into the lights and dashed away in long jolting leaps. And the dawn came up behind them ... and then — suddenly they saw the great valley below them. *(Morning light spreads slowly. A bird calls nearby.)*

AL. Jesus Christ! Look!

FIRST NARRATOR. The vineyards, the orchards, the great flat valley, green and beautiful, the trees set in rows, and the farm houses. *(Tom cuts the engine and the music stops.)*

PA. God Almighty!

AL. I want ta look at her. *(Al jumps out and stretches his legs. Pa climbs down with Tom. Ruthie and Winfield scramble around and climb into the cab, awestruck and embarrassed before the great valley.)*

PA. I never knowed they was anything like her.

AL. Ma — come look. It's California! We're there! *(Casy, Uncle John, Connie and Rose of Sharon climb down. They stand silently looking out.)*

TOM. Where's Ma? I want Ma to see it. Ma! *(Ma stumbles out from behind the truck.)* My God, Ma, you sick?

MA. Ya say we're acrost? *(Her face is putty-like. She holds on to the truck.)*

TOM. Look! *(She turns her head. Her mouth opens a little and her fingers go to her throat and gather a little pinch of skin.)*

MA. Thank God! The fambly's here. *(Her knees buckle.)*

TOM. You sick, Ma?

MA. No, jus' tar'd.

TOM. Was Granma bad? *(Ma raises her eyes and looks over at Pa and Uncle John.)*

MA. Granma's dead.

PA. When?

MA. Before they stopped us las' night.

PA. So that's why you didn't want 'em to look.

MA. I was afraid we wouldn't get acrost. I tol' Granma we couldn' he'p her. The fambly had to get acrost. She can get buried in a nice green place ... She got to lay her head down in California. *(They look at her in terror.)*

TOM. Jesus Christ! You layin' there with her all night long!

MA. The fambly hadda get acrost. *(Tom moves close to put his hand on her shoulder.)* Don't touch me. I'll hol' up if you don' touch me. That'd get me. *(Pa moves to her. Ma looks up at him. Casy turns to Uncle John.)*

CASY. All night long. John, there's a woman so great with love — she scares me. Makes me afraid an' mean.

MA. *(Looking out over the valley.)* It's purty. I wisht they could of saw it.

PA. I wisht so too.

TOM. They was too old. They wouldn't of saw nothin' that's here. Grampa would a been a-seein' the Injuns an' the prairie country when he was a young fella. An' Granma would a remembered an' seen the first home she lived in. They was too ol'. Who's really seein' it is Ruthie an' Winfiel'.

PA. Here's Tommy talkin' like a growed-up man, talkin' like a preacher almos'.

MA. He is. Growed way up — way up so I can't get ahold of 'im sometimes.

TOM. I guess we got to go to the coroner, wherever he is.

47

We got to get her buried decent. How much money might be lef', Pa?

PA. 'Bout forty dollars.

TOM. Jesus, are we gonna start clean! We sure ain't bringin' nothin' with us. (*Slowly the light fades. A bird calls faintly in the distance as the family looks out over the great flat valley.*)

CURTAIN

ACT II

In the dark, a jaw harp twangs. Campfires flare. Men, women and children huddle and shiver in the gloom. An infant cries. Dry coughs rise up with the feeble smoke. Rags hang on clotheslines. One man, Floyd Knowles, is grinding valves near his battered "Graham." His wife and baby are nearby. Another man is carefully preparing a baby for burial, slowly wrapping it in layer upon layer of fabrics and blankets. The Joads appear carrying bundles and wander through the camp. The huddled migrants barely notice. An old man with rolled-up pants, a bucket of water and an armload of bundles approaches Pa.

PA. Is it all right to set our stuff anywheres?

MAYOR OF HOOVERVILLE. Set down anywheres, here in this place?

PA. Sure. Anybody own this place, that we got to see 'fore we can camp? *(The old man squints.)*

MAYOR. You wanta camp here?

PA. What you think I'm a-sayin'?

MAYOR. Well, if you wanta camp here, why don't ya? I ain't a-stoppin' you.

PA. I jus' wanted to know does anybody own it? Do we got to pay?

MAYOR. Who owns it? *(Pa turns away.)*

PA. The hell with it. *(Al approaches Tom.)*

AL. Engine seems to be doin' awright, eh?

TOM. You done a nice job a pickin'. That what ya want me to say?

AL. Well, I sure was scairt the whole way, figgerin' she'd bust down an' it'd be my fault.

TOM. No, you done good. Better get her in shape, 'cause tomorra we're goin' out lookin' for work.

AL. She'll roll. Don't you worry none about that.

MAYOR. Who owns it? Who's gonna kick us outa here? You

49

tell *me*.

PA. You better go take a good long sleep. *(The old man wanders away.)*

TOM. What the hell was that? *(The man grinding valves looks up, his eyes are shiny with amusement.)*

FLOYD. H'are ya? I seen you just met the Mayor.

TOM. What the hell's the matter with 'im? *(Floyd chuckles.)*

FLOYD. He's jus' nuts like you an' me. Maybe he's a little nutser'n me, I don' know.

PA. I jus' ast him if we could camp here. *(Floyd wipes his greasy hands on his trousers.)*

FLOYD. Sure. Why not? You folks jus' come acrost?

TOM. Yeah. Jus' got in this mornin'.

FLOYD. Never been in Hooverville before?

TOM. Where's Hooverville?

FLOYD. This here's her. *(The Joad family begins to set up camp. Al crouches at his tool box. Ma and Uncle John set up the cooking tripod and pot of potatoes. Pa lays out a mattress. Rose of Sharon, Ruthie and Winfield huddle. Pa wanders away.)*

TOM. What the hell was the matter'th that ol' fella? *(Tom moves over to Floyd.)*

FLOYD. The Mayor? Chris' knows. I guess maybe he's bull-simple.

TOM. What's bull-simple? *(Floyd goes back to his work.)*

FLOYD. I guess cops push 'im aroun' so much he's still spinning.

TOM. Why would they push a fella like that aroun'? *(Floyd stops and looks at Tom.)*

FLOYD. Chris' knows. You jus' camps in one place a little while, an' you see how quick a deputy sheriff shoves you along.

TOM. But what the hell for?

FLOYD. I don't know. Some says they don' want us to vote; keep us movin' so we can't vote. An' some says so we can't get on relief. An' some says if we set in one place we'd get organized. I don' know why. I on'y know we got rode all the time. You wait, you'll see.

TOM. We ain't no bums. We're lookin' for work. We'll take any kind a work. *(Floyd looks at Tom in amazement. Uncle John*

drifts off.)
FLOYD. Lookin' for work? So you're lookin' for work. What ya think ever'body else is lookin' for? Di'monds? What you think I wore my ass down to a nub lookin' for?
TOM. Ain't they no work?
FLOYD. I don' know. Mus' be. Ain't no crop right here now. Grapes to pick later, an' cotton to pick later. We're a-movin' on, soon's I get these here valves groun'. Me an' my wife an' my kid. We heard they was work up north. We're shovin' north, up aroun' Salinas. *(Ma cuts potatoes at the fire.)*
TOM. Back home some fellas come through with han'bills — orange ones. Says they need lots a people out here to work the crops. *(Floyd laughs.)*
FLOYD. They say they's three hunderd thousan' us folks here, an' I bet ever' dam' fam'ly seen them han'bills.
TOM. But they is work. Christ Almighty, with all this stuff a-growin'; orchards, grapes, vegetables — I seen it. They got to have men. I seen all that stuff.
FLOYD. I'll tell ya. They's a big son-of-a-bitch of a peach orchard I worked in. Takes nine men all the year roun'. Takes three thousan' men for two weeks when them peaches is ripe. Got to have 'em or them peaches'll rot. So what do they do? They send out han'bills all over hell. They need three thousan', an' they get six thousan'. They get them men for what they wanta pay. If ya don' wanta take what they pay, goddamn it, they's a thousan' men waitin' for your job. *(A group of children gathers near Ma.)*
TOM. Them peaches got to be picked right now, don't they? Jus' when they're ripe?
FLOYD. 'Course they do. *(The children watch Ma's hands.)*
TOM. Well, s'pose them people got together an' says, "Let 'em rot." Wouldn' be long 'fore the price went up, by God! *(Floyd looks up.)*
FLOYD. Well, you figgered out somepin', didn' you. Come right outa your own head.
TOM. I'm tar'd. Drove all night. I don' wanta start no argument. An' I'm so goddamn tar'd I'd argue easy. Don' be smart with me. I'm askin' you. *(A harmonica murmurs in the dark. Floyd*

51

and Tom stoop close together. Casy wanders through the camp.)
FLOYD. I didn' mean it. You ain't been here. Folks figgered
that out. An' the folks with the peach orchard figgered her out
too. Look, if the folks get together, they's a leader — got to
be — fella that does the talkin'. Well, first time this fella opens
his mouth they grab 'im an' stick 'im in jail. An' if they's
another leader pops up, why they stick *'im* in jail.
TOM. Well, a fella eats in jail anyways.
FLOYD. His kids don't. How'd you like to be in an' your kids
starvin' to death? *(Tom takes off his cap and twists it in his hands.*
Casy is stretched out some distance away. He has removed one shoe
and is contemplating his big toe.)
TOM. Yeah. Yeah. So we take what we can get, huh, or we
starve; an' if we yelp we starve. I ain't gonna take it. *(He looks*
over at his mother scraping potatoes. The circle of children has drawn
closer.) Goddamn it, I an' my folks ain't no sheep. I'll kick the
hell outa somebody.
FLOYD. Like a cop?
TOM. Like anybody.
FLOYD. You're nuts. They'll pick you right off. You got no
name, no property. They'll find you in a ditch, with the blood
dried on your mouth an' your nose. Be one little line in the
paper — know what it'll say? "Vagrant foun' dead." An' that's
all. You'll see a lot of them little lines, "Vagrant foun' dead."
TOM. They'll be somebody else foun' dead right 'longside of
this here vagrant.
FLOYD. You're nuts. Won't be no good in that. *(Floyd goes*
back to his seat and continues working on the valves. Tom stands.
Rose of Sharon runs off. Connie follows her.)
TOM. *(Under his breath.)* Bull-simple. *(He approaches Casy and*
stands above and behind him.) Think she's gonna work? *(He sits*
down.)
CASY. What?
TOM. Them toes of yourn.
CASY. Oh! Jus' settin' here a-thinkin'.
TOM. You always get good an' comf'table for it. *(Casy waggles*
his big toe.)
CASY. Hard enough for a fella to think 'thout kinkin' hisself

up to do it.

TOM. Ain't heard a peep outa you for days. Thinkin' all the time?

CASY. Yeah, thinkin' all the time. *(Tom takes off his cap, turns out the sweatband and removes a long strip of folded newspaper. Casy turns his head.)*

TOM. Sweat so much she's shrank. Could ya come down from your thinkin' an' listen a minute?

CASY. Listen all the time. That's why I been thinkin'. Listen to people a-talkin', an' purty soon I hear the way folks are feelin'. Goin' on all the time. I hear 'em an' feel 'em; an' they're beating their wings like a bird in a attic. Gonna bust their wings on a dusty winda tryin' ta get out. *(Tom regards him with wide eyes.)*

TOM. That was about what I was gonna tell ya. An' you seen awready. *(Casy bows his head and runs his hand through his hair.)*

CASY. I seen. They's a army of us without no harness. All along I seen it. Ever' place we stopped I seen it. Folks hungry for side-meat, an' when they get it, they ain't fed. An' when they'd get so hungry they couldn' stan' it no more, why, they'd ast me to pray for 'em, an' sometimes I done it. I use ta think that'd cut 'er. Use ta rip off a prayer an' all the troubles'd stick to that prayer like flies on fly paper, an' the prayer'd go a-sailin' off, a-takin' them troubles along. But it don' work no more.

TOM. Prayer never brought in no side-meat. Takes a shoat to bring in pork.

CASY. Yeah. An' Almighty God never raised no wages. These here folks want to live decent and bring up their kids decent. An' when they're old they wanta set in the door an' watch the downing sun. An' when they're young they wanta dance an' sing an' lay together. They wanta eat an' get drunk and work. An' that's it — they wanta jus' fling their goddamn muscles aroun' an' get tired. Christ! What'm I talkin' about?

TOM. I dunno. Sounds kinda nice. When ya think you can get ta work an' quit thinkin' a spell? We got to get work. Money's 'bout gone. Pa give five dollars to get a painted piece of board stuck up over Granma. We ain't got much lef'.

CASY. I ain't doin' nobody no good. Me or nobody else. I was thinkin' I'd go off alone by myself. I'm a-eatin' your food an' a-takin' up room. An' I ain't give you nothin'. Maybe I could get a steady job an' maybe pay back some a the stuff you've give me. *(Tom stares out over the camp.)*

TOM. Wisht I had a sack a Durham. I ain't had a smoke in a hell of a time. Use'ta get tobacco in McAlester. Almost wish I was back. Ever been in a jail house?

CASY. No. Never been. Why?

TOM. When you're in jail — you get to kinda — sensin' stuff. Guys ain't let to talk a hell of a lot together — two maybe, but not a crowd. An' so you get kinda sensy. If somepin's gonna bust — you know before it happens. An' if they's gonna be a break or a riot, nobody don't have to tell ya. You're sensy about it. You know.

CASY. Yeah?

TOM. Don't go away right yet. Not right yet. *(Casy waves his toes up and down and studies them gravely. Tom settles back on his elbow and closes his eyes. Rose of Sharon runs on followed by Connie. Connie grabs her and spins her around.)*

CONNIE. If I'd of knowed it would be like this I wouldn' of came. I'd a studied nights 'bout tractors back home an' got me a three-dollar job. Fella can live awful nice on three dollars a day, an' go to the pitcher show ever'night, too.

ROSE OF SHARON. You're gonna study nights 'bout radios. Ain't you?

CONNIE. Yeah, sure. Soon's I get on my feet. Get a little money.

ROSE OF SHARON. You ain't givin' it up!

CONNIE. No — no — 'course not. But — I didn' know they was places like this we got to live in. *(Her eyes harden.)*

ROSE OF SHARON. You got to.

CONNIE. Sure. Sure, I know. Got to get on my feet. Get a little money. Would a been better to stay home an' study 'bout tractors. Three dollars a day they get, an' pick up extra money, too. But I'm gonna study. Soon's I get on my feet.

ROSE OF SHARON. We got to have a house 'fore the baby comes. We ain't gonna have this baby in no tent.

CONNIE. Sure. Soon's I get on my feet. *(Rose of Sharon runs away and Connie follows. Pa moves down to the Joad camp. Al strolls over to watch Floyd at his valve-grinding job. Ma stands up at the fire, and gives the watching children something to eat. They run back to their own camps ravenously eating the tiny morsels.)*

AL. Looks like you're 'bout through.

FLOYD. Two more.

AL. Any girls in this here camp?

FLOYD. I got a wife. I got no time for girls.

AL. I always got time for girls. I got no time for nothin' else.

FLOYD. You get a little hungry an' you'll change. *(Al laughs. Uncle John moves to the Joad camp. A man dressed in khaki trousers, a jacket, and a flannel shirt appears. He moves through the camp passing out handbills.)*

AL. Maybe. But I ain't never changed that notion yet.

FLOYD. Fella I talked to while ago, he's with you, ain't he?

AL. Yeah! My brother Tom. Better not fool with him. He killed a fella.

FLOYD. Did? What for?

AL. Fight. Fella got a knife in Tom. Tom busted 'im with a shovel.

FLOYD. Did, huh? What'd the law do?

AL. Let 'im off 'cause it was a fight.

FLOYD. He don't look like a quarreler.

AL. Oh, he ain't. But Tom don't take nothin' from nobody. Tom, he's quiet. But — look out!

FLOYD. Well — I talked to 'im. He didn' soun' mean.

AL. Like me to he'p you get them valves set an' the head on?

FLOYD. Well, I'd admire to git a hand. My name's Floyd Knowles.

AL. I'm Al Joad.

FLOYD. Proud to meet ya.

AL. Jesus! They ain't nothin' I love like the guts of a engine.

FLOYD. How 'bout girls?

AL. Yeah, girls too! *(He wipes his hands on his trousers. Floyd moves over to meet the contractor. Other men emerge and gather. Tom and Casy move up to join the Joad family.)*

CONTRACTOR. You men want to work?

MAN IN CROWD. Sure we wanta work. *(Floyd steps out ahead of the others.)*

FLOYD. *(Quietly.)* I'll go mister. You're a contractor, an' you got a license. You jus' show your license, an' then you gives us an order to go work, an' where, an' when, an' how much we'll get, an' you sign that, an' we'll all go. *(The contractor turns.)*

CONTRACTOR. You telling me how to run my own business?

FLOYD. 'F we're workin' for you, it's our business too.

CONTRACTOR. Well, you ain't telling me what to do. Fruits opening up. I need men.

FLOYD. But you ain't sayin' how many men, an' you ain't sayin' what you'd pay.

CONTRACTOR. Goddamn it, I don't know yet.

FLOYD. If you don' know, you got no right to hire men.

CONTRACTOR. I got a right to run my business my own way. If you men want to sit here on your ass, OK. I'm getting men for Tulare County. Going to need a lot of men. *(Floyd turns to the crowd of men.)*

FLOYD. Twicet now I've fell for that. Maybe he needs a thousan' men. He'll get five thousan' there, an' he'll pay fifteen cents an hour. An' you poor bastards'll have to take it 'cause you'll be hungry. 'F he wants to hire men, let him hire 'em an' write it out an' say what he's gonna pay. Ast ta see his license. He ain't allowed to contract without a license. *(A man appears, on his leather jacket is pinned the star of the deputy sheriff. A heavy pistol holster hangs on his belt. He moves through the crowd.)*

CONTRACTOR. Ever see this guy before, Joe?

DEPUTY SHERIFF. Which one?

CONTRACTOR. *(Indicating Floyd.)* This fella.

DEPUTY SHERIFF. What'd he do?

CONTRACTOR. He's talking red, agitating trouble.

DEPUTY SHERIFF. Hm-m-m. *(He moves slowly around Floyd.)*

FLOYD. You see? If this guy's on the level, would he bring a cop along?

CONTRACTOR. Ever see 'im before?

DEPUTY SHERIFF. Hmmm, seems like I have. Las' week

when that used-car lot was busted into. Seems like I seen this fella hangin' aroun'. Yep! I'd swear it's the same fella. You come on. *(He unhooks the strap that covers the butt of his automatic.)*

TOM. You got nothin' on him. *(The deputy swings around, and moves slowly to Tom.)*

DEPUTY SHERIFF. 'F you'd like to go in too, you jus' open your trap once more. They was two fellas hangin' around that lot.

TOM. I wasn't even in the State las' week.

DEPUTY SHERIFF. Well, maybe you're wanted someplace else. You keep your trap shut, Okie. *(The deputy gives Tom a sudden violent shove. The contractor turns back to the men.)*

CONTRACTOR. You fellas don't want ta listen to these goddamn reds. Trouble-makers — they'll get you in trouble. Now I can use all of you in Tulare County. *(The men are silent. The deputy smiles.)*

DEPUTY SHERIFF. Might be a good idear to go. Board of Health says we got to clean out this camp. An' if it gets around that you got reds out here — why, somebody might git hurt. Be a good idear if all you fellas moved on to Tulare. They isn't a thing to do aroun' here. That's jus' a friendly way a telling you. Be a bunch a guys down here, maybe with pick handles, if you ain't gone. *(Ma and Ruthie appear near the Joad camp.)*

CONTRACTOR. I told you I need men. If you don't want to work — well, that's your business. *(Floyd stands stiffly, his thumbs hooked over his belt. The contractor moves away.)*

DEPUTY SHERIFF. *(Moving to Floyd.)* Now c'mon, Hayseed, we're goin for a ride. *(Floyd's wife tries to intercede, but Al holds her back. The deputy reaches a large hand up and takes hold of Floyd's left arm. Floyd pushes the hand away. The deputy reaches again and Floyd pushes the hand away again and swings with one movement. His fist splashes into the large face, and in the same motion he is away. The deputy falls in a heap on the ground. Floyd bumps into Casy, who sends him off. The deputy stands, draws his gun, and moves after Floyd, who pushes through the crowd.)*

AL. He's got a gun! *(Tom steps in and puts out his foot. The deputy falls heavily and rolls, looking back at Tom. The crowd screams and parts at the sight of the deputy's gun. Floyd trips and falls to the ground. The deputy fires. A woman near Floyd screams and grabs her hand. Floyd stands and ducks out of sight. The deputy, kneeling on the ground, raises his gun again and then, suddenly, from the group of men, Casy steps in. He kicks the deputy in the face and then stands back as the heavy man crumples. Most of the crowd flees. The deputy is lying on his back, his mouth open. Tom picks up his automatic and pulls out the magazine. Casy kneels down and checks the deputy.)*

TOM. Fella like that ain't got no right to a gun. *(A small crowd gathers around the wounded woman. Ma moves to her. Casy moves close to Tom, takes the gun and places it next to the deputy.)*

CASY. You got to git out. You go down in the willas an' wait. He didn't see me kick 'im, but he seen you stick out your foot.

TOM. I don' want ta go.

CASY. They'll fingerprint you. You broke parole. They'll send you back.

TOM. Jesus! I forgot.

CASY. Go quick. 'Fore he comes to. *(Tom runs away. Al steps over to the fallen deputy, then turns to Casy admiringly.)*

AL. Jesus, you sure flagged 'im down!

CASY. *(To Al.)* Get out. Go on, get out — to the fambly. You don't know nothin'.

AL. Yeah? How 'bout you?

CASY. *(To the family.)* Somebody got to take the blame. I got no kids. They'll jus' put me in jail, an' I ain't doin' nothin' but set aroun'.

AL. Ain't no reason for —

CASY. Go on now. You get outa this.

AL. *(Bristling.)* I ain't takin' orders.

CASY. If you mess in this your whole fambly, all your folks, gonna get in trouble. I don' care about you. But your ma and your pa, they'll get in trouble. Maybe they'll send Tom back to McAlester.

AL. OK. I think you're a damn fool, though.

CASY. Sure. Why not? *(Al runs over to the family as Casy kneels*

58

beside the deputy. The deputy groans. Two armed men run on. Casy stands up.)

OFFICER. What the hell's goin' on here? *(He goes to the deputy who is trying to sit up. The second officer picks up the deputy's gun. Connie appears.)*

CASY. I knocked out your man there.

OFFICER. Now what happened here?

CASY. Well, he got tough an' I hit 'im, and he started shootin' — hit a woman over there. So I hit 'im again. *(The deputy stands up slowly.)*

OFFICER. Well, what'd you do in the first place?

CASY. I talked back.

OFFICER. Awright, you're going with me.

CASY. Sure. They's a woman over there like to bleed to death from his bad shootin'.

OFFICER. We'll see about that later. Joe, is this the fella that hit you? *(The deputy stares sickly at Casy.)*

DEPUTY SHERIFF. Don't look like him.

CASY. It was me all right. You got smart with the wrong fella.

DEPUTY SHERIFF. You don't look like the right fella to me. By God, I'm gonna be sick! *(The deputy stumbles away. Connie runs off as the officer approaches.)*

CASY. I'll go 'thout no trouble. You better see how bad that woman's hurt. *(The first officer puts handcuffs on Casy and then leads him away. Uncle John and Pa watch. Al runs off.)*

PA. Now what the hell made the preacher do that?

UNCLE JOHN. He knowed about sin. I ast him about sin, an' he tol' me; but I don't know if he's right. He says a fella's sinned if he thinks he's sinned. I been secret all my days. I done things I never tol' about.

MA. *(Turning from the fire.)* Don' go tellin', John, Tell 'em to God. Don' go burdenin' other people with your sins. That ain't decent.

UNCLE JOHN. They're a-eatin' on me.

MA. Well, don' tell 'em. Go down the river an' stick your head under an' whisper 'em in the stream.

UNCLE JOHN. I got to tell.

PA. Well, then goddamn it! Who'd ya kill? *(Uncle John digs with*

59

his thumb into the watch pocket of his blue jeans and scoops out a folded dirty bill.)

UNCLE JOHN. Fi' dollars.

PA. Steal her?

UNCLE JOHN. No, I had her. Kept her out. *(Rose of Sharon appears, searching for Connie.)*

PA. She was yourn, wasn't she?

UNCLE JOHN. Yeah, but I didn't have no right to keep her out. *(Rose of Sharon wanders away.)*

MA. I don't see much sin in that. It's yourn.

UNCLE JOHN. It ain't only the keepin' her out. I kep' her out to get drunk. I knowed they was gonna come a time when I got to get drunk, when I'd get to hurtin' inside so I got to get drunk. Figgered time wasn't yet, an' then — the preacher went and give 'imself up to save Tom.

MA. I don' see why him savin' Tom got to get you drunk.

UNCLE JOHN. Can't say her. Look! You got the money. Gimme two dollars. *(Pa reaches in his pocket and brings out a leather pouch.)*

PA. You ain't gonna need no seven dollars to get drunk. You don't need to drink champagny water.

UNCLE JOHN. *(Holding out his bill.)* Take this here an' gimme two dollars. I can get good an' drunk for two dollars. I don' want no sin of waste on me. I'll spend whatever I got. Always do. *(Pa takes the dirty bill and gives Uncle John two silver dollars.)*

PA. There ya are. A fella got to do what he got to do. Nobody don' know enough to tell 'im.

UNCLE JOHN. You ain't gonna be mad? You know I got to?

PA. Christ, yes. You know what you got to do. *(Uncle John walks forlornly away. Rose of Sharon appears.)*

ROSE OF SHARON. Where's Connie? I ain't seen Connie for a long time. Where'd he go?

MA. I ain't seen him. If I see 'im, I'll tell 'im you want 'im.

ROSE OF SHARON. I ain't feelin' good. Connie shouldn' of left me. *(Ma looks at the girl's swollen face.)*

MA. You been a-cryin'. You git aholt on yaself. They's a lot of us here. Come here now an' peel some potatoes. You're feelin' sorry for yaself.

ROSE OF SHARON. He shouldn' of went away.

MA. You got to work. I ain't had time to take you in han'. I will now. You take this here knife an' get to them potatoes. *(Rose of Sharon takes the knife from Ma and sits at the fire.)*

ROSE OF SHARON. Wait'll I see 'im. I'll tell 'im.

MA. He might smack you. You got it comin' with whinin' aroun' an' candyin' yaself. If he smacks some sense in you I'll bless 'im. *(Rose of Sharon's eyes blaze. Ma and Pa move away. Tom and Al run on.)*

TOM. Casy shouldn' of did it. I might of knew, though. He was talkin' how he ain't done nothin' for us. He's a funny fella, Al. All the time thinkin'.

AL. Comes from bein' a preacher. They get all messed up with stuff.

TOM. Where ya s'pose Connie was a-goin'?

AL. Goin' to take a crap, I guess.

TOM. Well, he was goin' a hell of a long way. *(Floyd runs on and meets them.)*

FLOYD. You gettin' out?

TOM. I don't know. Think we better? *(Floyd laughs.)*

FLOYD. You heard what that bull said. They'll burn ya out if ya don't. 'F you think that guy's gonna take a beatin' 'thout gettin' back, you're nuts. The pool-room boys'll be down here tonight to burn us out. *(Floyd and his wife begin breaking up their camp.)*

TOM. Guess we better git, then. Where you a-goin'?

FLOYD. Why, up north, I guess.

TOM. So long, Floyd.

FLOYD. So long. Prob'ly see you. Hope so.

AL. Good-by. *(Floyd and his wife hurry away, pushing their Graham out of sight. Ma appears.)*

MA. It's Tom! Thank God.

TOM. We got to get outa here. *(Pa approaches.)*

MA. What's the matter now?

TOM. Well, Floyd says they'll burn the camp tonight.

PA. What the hell for? We ain't done nothin'.

61

TOM. Nothin' 'cept beat up a cop.

PA. Well, we never done it.

TOM. From what that cop said, they wanta push along.

ROSE OF SHARON. *(To Al.)* You seen Connie?

AL. Yeah. Way to hell an' gone up the river. He's goin' south.

ROSE OF SHARON. Was — was he goin' away?

AL. I don' know. *(Ma turns to Rose of Sharon.)*

MA. Rosasharn, you been talkin' an' actin' funny. What'd Connie say to you?

ROSE OF SHARON. Said it would a been a good thing if he stayed home an' studied up tractors. *(Rose of Sharon's eyes glisten in the firelight.)*

PA. Connie wasn't no good. I seen that a long time. Didn' have no guts, jus' too big for his overhalls.

AL. Wouldn' do no good to catch 'im, I guess.

PA. No. If he ain't no good, we don't want him.

MA. Sh. Don' say that.

PA. Well, he ain't no good. All the time a-sayin' what he's a-gonna do. Never doin' nothin'. *(Rose of Sharon throws the knife into the potato pot and runs off.)* I didn't want to say nothin' while he's here. But now he's run out —

MA. Sh!

PA. Why, for Christ's sake? Why do I got to "sh"? He run out, didn' he?

MA. Rosasharn's gonna have a little fella an' that baby is half Connie. It ain't good for a baby to grow up with folks a-sayin' his pa ain't no good.

PA. Better'n lyin' about it.

MA. No, it ain't. Make out like he's dead. You wouldn' say no bad things about Connie if he's dead.

TOM. Hey, what is this? We ain't sure Connie's gone for good. We got no time for talkin'. We got to get on our way.

MA. On our way? We jus' come here.

TOM. They gonna burn the camp tonight, Ma. Now you know I ain't got it in me to stan' by an' see our stuff burn up, nor Pa ain't got it in him, nor Uncle John. We'd come up a-fightin', and I jus' can't afford to be took in an' mugged. I nearly got it today, if the preacher hadn' jumped in.

MA. Come on! We got to be quick.

TOM. Al, go get the truck. *(Al runs off. Ma, Pa, Ruthie and Winfield start to pack up the camp.)*

PA. How 'bout John?

TOM. Where's Uncle John?

PA. He went to get drunk.

TOM. Jesus! Look, you all get the stuff loaded. I'll go look for Uncle John. *(He walks quickly away. Ma, Pa, Ruthie and Winfield gather up the cooking stuff and the mattress. The fiddle fills the night with soft melody. Uncle John appears nursing his bottle and dancing.)*

UNCLE JOHN. Yes sir, she was a girl with pretty feet, and she danced one time... *(The truck, with Al at the wheel, moves on and stops. Tom runs on and approaches Uncle John.)*

TOM. Come on, Uncle John...

UNCLE JOHN. Tom, ought to find a girl to talk to.

TOM. Sure, John...

UNCLE JOHN. Might lay with her, too.

TOM. Come on now, Uncle John.

UNCLE JOHN. Like to stay drunk all the time. *(The Joads have loaded the truck. Ruthie and Winfield climb on.)*

AL. He sure got a quick start.

TOM. He's like you, Al, been out lookin' for girls. Poor fella. *(Pa appears and helps Uncle John into the back of the truck.)*

PA. Awready.

TOM. Where's Rosasharn?

MA. Over there. *(Rose of Sharon appears with a carpetbag.)* Come on, Rosasharn. We're a-goin'.

ROSE OF SHARON. I ain't a-goin'. *(She kneels with her bag.)*

TOM. You got to go.

ROSE OF SHARON. I want Connie. I ain't a-goin' till he comes back.

TOM. Connie'll find us. *(Ma approaches.)*

MA. Come on, Rosasharn. Come on, honey.

ROSE OF SHARON. I wanta wait.

MA. We can't wait. *(Ma leans down, takes Rose of Sharon by the arm, and helps her to her feet.)*

TOM. He'll find us. Don' you worry. He'll find us.

ROSE OF SHARON. Maybe he went to get them books to study up. Maybe he was a-gonna surprise us.

MA. Maybe that's jus' what he done. *(Ma leads her to the truck and helps her up on the load. Tom move to Pa. The Mayor of Hooverville wanders on and approaches the men.)*

MAYOR. You gonna leave any stuff a fella could use?

PA. Can't think of nothin'. We ain't got nothin' to leave.

TOM. Ain't ya gettin' out?

MAYOR. No.

TOM. But they'll burn ya out.

MAYOR. I know. They done it before.

TOM. Well, why the hell don't ya get out?

MAYOR. I don't know. Takes so long to git stuff together. *(He wanders vaguely away.)*

PA. What's a matter with him?

TOM. Cop-happy. Fella was sayin' — he's bull-simple. Been beat over the head too much. Come on, Pa. Let's go. Look here, Pa. You an' me an' Al ride in the seat. Ma can get on the load. No, Ma, you ride in the middle. *(He moves to the truck and picks up a monkey wrench from the toolbox.)* Al, you get up behind. Take this here. *(He hands Al the wrench.)* Jus' in case. If anybody tries to climb up — let 'im have it. *(Al climbs in the back of the truck.)*

PA. I ain't got nothin' in my han'.

TOM. *(Exploding.)* Well reach over an' get the jack handle! *(Pa moves slowly around the truck, shaking his head. Tom watches, and then moves away. Ma follows.)* There comes a time when a man gets mad.

MA. Tom — you tol' me — you promised me you wasn't like that. You promised.

TOM. I know, Ma. I'm a-tryin'. But them deputies — Ma, if it was the law they was workin' with, why, we could take it. But it *ain't* the law. They're a-workin' away at our spirits. They're a-tryin' to make us cringe an' crawl like a whipped bitch. They tryin' to break us. Why, Jesus Christ, Ma, they comes a time when the on'y way a fella can keep his decency is by takin' a sock at a cop. They're workin' on our decency.

MA. You promised, Tom.

TOM. I'm a-tryin', Ma. Honest to God, I am. You don' want me to crawl like a beat bitch, with my belly on the groun', do you?

MA. I'm a-prayin'. You got to keep clear, Tom. The fambly's breakin' up. You got to keep clear.

TOM. I'll try, Ma. But when one a them fat asses gets to workin' me over, I got a big job tryin'. If it was the law, it's be different. But burnin' the camp ain't the law.

MA. Easy. You got to have patience. Why, Tom — us people will go on livin' when all them people is gone. Why, Tom, we're the people that live. They ain't gonna wipe us out. Why, we're the people — we go on.

TOM. We take a beatin' all the time.

MA. But, Tom, we keep a-comin'. Don' you fret none, Tom. A different time's comin'.

TOM. How do you know?

MA. I don't know.

TOM. Never heard you talk so much in my life. (*They move to the truck. Tom hops behind the wheel. The truck moves across the expanse of wood and dust, then drives off as darkness approaches. Fire crackles and roars in the distance. Deputies with lanterns and guns move through the dark shouting. The Mayor wanders through the abandoned camp pulling a red wagon loaded with junk. All but one of the men with laterns disperse. The single lantern is held high, its circle of light spreads revealing Tom and the Weedpatch Camp Direc-tor. A sign above reads:*

WEEDPATCH CAMP
OPERATED BY THE U.S. GOVERNMENT)

WEEDPATCH CAMP DIRECTOR. The camp site costs a dollar a week, but you can work it out, carrying garbage, keeping the camp clean — stuff like that. It's a nice place. Folks that had it just moved out.

TOM. We'll work it out.

WEEDPATCH CAMP DIRECTOR. You'll see the committee Monday mornin'.

TOM. Cops?

WEEDPATCH CAMP DIRECTOR. No cops. We got our own cops. Folks here elects a committee that makes the laws. What they say goes.

TOM. You mean to say the fellas that runs the camp is jus' fellas — campin' here?

WEEDPATCH CAMP DIRECTOR. Sure, and it works.

TOM. You mean they ain't no cops?

WEEDPATCH CAMP DIRECTOR. No, sir. No cop can come in here without a warrant.

TOM. God Almighty, I can't hardly believe it! Last night them deputies, they burned the camp over by the river.

WEEDPATCH CAMP DIRECTOR. They don't get in here. Some nights, the boys patrol the fences, 'specially dance nights.

TOM. Dance nights? Well, Christ's sake! Why ain't they more places like this?

WEEDPATCH CAMP DIRECTOR. You'll have to find that out for yourself. *(Al appears in the distance.)*

AL. Gonna stay here?

TOM. Yeah. Y'all unload the truck. I got to go to the office.

WEEDPATCH CAMP DIRECTOR. Come along, Mr. Joad. *(Al runs off. Rose of Sharon appears. She wanders through the great empty space under the sign caressing her huge belly. The Camp Director walks briskly away. Tom follows. Ma and the children file on and meet a group of women. Rose of Sharon moves slowly into the foreground. The women distribute blankets, soap and toilet paper to Ma and the children, then lead them gently away. Elizabeth Sandry emerges out of the shadows carrying an apple box full of laundry. She notices Rose of Sharon caressing herself.)*

ELIZABETH SANDRY. So! What do you think it's gonna be?

ROSE OF SHARON. I don' know.

ELIZABETH SANDRY. Got a live tumor. Which'd you ruther?

ROSE OF SHARON. I dunno — boy, I guess. Sure — boy.

ELIZABETH SANDRY. You jus' come in, didn' ya?

ROSE OF SHARON. Uh-huh.

ELIZABETH SANDRY. Gonna stay?

ROSE OF SHARON. I don' know. 'F we can get work, guess we will.

ELIZABETH SANDRY. 'F you can git work. That's what we all say.

ROSE OF SHARON. My brother says he might a get a job

right away!

ELIZABETH SANDRY. That's what he says, huh? Maybe he will. Maybe you're lucky. Look out for luck. You cain't trust luck. You cain't have but one kind of luck. Cain't have more. You be a good girl. *(Fiercely.)* You be good. If you got sin on you — you better watch out for that there baby. They's scandalous things goes on in this here camp... *(A fiddle begins to tune up for a square dance. Musicians appear and set up their instruments and a microphone. People gather in the shadows around them.)*

ROSE OF SHARON. Is?

ELIZABETH SANDRY. You let me warn you now. They ain't but a few deep down Jesus-lovers lef'. Every Sat'dy night when that there strang ban' starts up an' should be a'playin hymnody, they're a-reelin' — yes, sir, a-reelin'! An' don' you think them sinners is puttin' nothin' over on God, neither. No, sir, He's a-chalkin' 'em up sin by sin. God's a-watchin', an' I'm a-watchin'! He's awready smoked one of 'em out. *(Ma appears in the distance with an old cigar box.)*

ROSE OF SHARON. Has?

ELIZABETH SANDRY. I seen it. A girl a-carryin' a little one, jes' like you. An' she hug-danced. An' she thinned out and she skinnied out, an' — she dropped that baby, dead.

ROSE OF SHARON. Oh, my.

ELIZABETH SANDRY. You take heed a that pore chile in your belly an' keep outa sin. *(Rose of Sharon moves away a little.)*

ROSE OF SHARON. *(To herself.)* I done it. I hug-danced. I done it in Sallisaw. Me an' Connie.

ELIZABETH SANDRY. I warned you. *(Ma steps between them.)*

MA. Howdy. *(Rose of Sharon swings around.)*

ROSE OF SHARON. Ma, this lady says...

ELIZABETH SANDRY. *(To Ma.)* Howdy. I'm Mis' Sandry. 'Lisbeth Sandry.

MA. Howdy do.

ELIZABETH SANDRY. Are you happy in the Lord?

MA. Pretty happy.

ELIZABETH SANDRY. Are you saved?

MA. I been saved.

ELIZABETH SANDRY. Well, I'm glad. The sinners is awful strong aroun' here. You come to a awful place. They's wicketness all around about. Wicket people, wicket goin's-on that lamb'-blood Christians jes' cain't hardly stan'. Wicket people!

MA. Seems to me they's nice people here.

ELIZABETH SANDRY. They's sinners all around us! *(Ma moves slowly to the woman and then explodes.)*

MA. Git! Git out now, 'fore I git to be a sinner a-tellin' you where to go.

ELIZABETH SANDRY. I thought you was Christians.

MA. So we are.

ELIZABETH SANDRY. No, you ain't. You're hell-burnin sinners, all of you! I can see your soul a-burnin'.

MA. Git! Don' you never come back. I seen your kind before. You'd take the little pleasure, wouldn' you?

ELIZABETH SANDRY. I can see that innocent child in that there girl's belly a-burnin'! *(A desparate cry escapes from Rose of Sharon. Ma advances on the woman, who backs away and runs off. The Camp Director signals the band, and they start to play. Couples move into their positions and begin to square dance.)*

MAN WITH GUITAR. *(Spoken in rhythm.)* Fiddle is rare, hard to learn! *(Singing.)*
> Fiddle is rare, hard to learn.
> No frets, no teacher.
> She ain't much of a fiddle. Paid two dollars.
> Heard of fiddles four hundred years old.
> They get mellow like whiskey.
> Says they cost fifty-sixty thousan' dollars.
> I don't know. Soun's like a lie.
> Harsh old bastard ain't she?
> Wanta dance?

(The Weedpatch Camp Director takes over the microphone. The dancing becomes wild and ecstatic. Al and a young girl swirl among the others.)

WEEDPATCH CAMP DIRECTOR. *(Calling.)* "Chicken Reel" now, and the feet tap. Square closes up and the dancing starts, feet on the bare groun', beating dull, strike with your heels. Hands 'round and swing. Hair falls down, and panting breaths.

Lean to the side now. Look at that Oklahoma boy! Long legs loose, taps four times for ever' damn step. Never seen a boy swing aroun' like that. Look at him swing that Cherokee girl, red in her cheeks an' her toe points out. Look at her pant, look at her heave. Think she's tired? Think she's winded? Well, she ain't. *(The music subsides but continues. A gentle waltz emerges. Couples begin "hug-dancin'." Al pulls the girl away from the others. Ma holds up a pair of gold earrings.)*

MA. Look. These is for you.

ROSE OF SHARON. I ain't pierced. *(Ma hands Rose of Sharon the earrings and opens the box.)*

MA. Well, I'm a-gonna pierce ya. *(She threads a needle.)*

ROSE OF SHARON. It'll hurt. It'll hurt. *(Al and the girl sit some distance away. Al attempts to kiss her.)*

AL'S GIRL. Don't. You tickle.

AL. I aim to.

AL'S GIRL. We're gonna git married, ain't we?

AL. Sure, sometime.

AL'S GIRL. I thought you said purty soon!

AL. Well, soon is when soon comes.

AL'S GIRL. You promised. You said we was.

AL. Well, sure we are. *(They kiss.)*

AL'S GIRL. You gettin' a job soon?

AL. You'll see. I'll have a pocketful of jack. We'll go down to Hollywood and see the pitchers. *(They kiss again. Ma clips with a small scissors at the threads hanging from Rose of Sharon's ears.)*

MA. It's all done. Now, ever' day we'll pull one knot, and in a couple weeks it'll be all well an' you can wear 'em. Here — they're your'n now. You can keep 'em. *(Rose of Sharon touches her ears tenderly and looks at the tiny spots of blood on her fingers.)*

ROSE OF SHARON. It didn' hurt. Jus' stuck a little.

MA. You oughta been pierced long ago. *(She smiles in triumph.)* Now let's get to the dancin'. Your baby gonna be a good baby. Very near let you have a baby without your ears was pierced. But you're safe now.

ROSE OF SHARON. Does it mean somepin'?

MA. Why, 'course it does. 'Course it does. *(Tom approaches Ma, takes her hand and leads her in the waltz. Al and his girl join the dancing. Rose of Sharon remains, touching her ear lobes gently. A lean man emerges from among the dancers and stands watching Ma and Tom dance. Ma and Tom are in one pool of light, the Third Narrator in another. As the Third Narrator speaks Ma and Tom slowly move away followed by Rose of Sharon. Al and his girl say goodbye and also move away.)*

THIRD NARRATOR.   The moving, questing people were migrants now. Those families which had lived on a little piece of land, who had lived and died on forty acres, had now the whole West to rove. And they scampered about, looking for work; and the highways were streams of people, and the ditch banks were lines of people. Behind them more were coming. *(Pa approaches the narrator and steps into the circle of light.)*

PA.   *(To the man.)* We're a-gettin' out in the morning.

THIRD NARRATOR.   Yeah?   Which way you goin'?

PA.   Thought we'd go up north a little. Fella came by las' night says there might be work pickin' peaches. We ain't had work. We're outa food. Folks been so nice here, and we had a bath ever' day. Never been so clean in my life. We hate to go, but there just ain't no work. *(They shake hands. Pa moves away. The sign disappears. The guitar plays. The dancers form a line silhouetted against the sky. The Joads are gone.)*

THIRD NARRATOR.   The Joads moved north, and the orchards lined the way and made an aisle. At the Hooper Ranch there were lines of men standing in the ditch beside the road. *(An iron fence is lowered in front of the frozen silhouette.)*

MAN WITH GUITAR.   *(Singing.)*

> In the eyes of the people
> There is a growing wrath.

(The light changes suddenly and the crowd becomes animated, yelling and taunting as men with rifles lead the Joads into position behind the iron fence. A man with a notebook appears in front of the fence. He flips a few pages and produces a pencil. One of the armed guards shoots his rifle in the air. The crowd is suddenly silent. The sound of crickets fills the night air as the crowd begins slowly to disperse.)

BOOKKEEPER.   Want to work?

TOM.   Sure, what is this?   All this commotion.

BOOKKEEPER. That's not your affair. Want to work?

TOM. Sure we do.

BOOKKEEPER. Name?

TOM. Joad.

BOOKKEEPER. How many men?

TOM. Four.

BOOKKEEPER. Women?

TOM. Two.

BOOKKEEPER. Kids?

TOM. Two.

BOOKKEEPER. Can all of you work?

TOM. Why — I guess so.

BOOKKEEPER. OK. Find house sixty-three. Wages five cents a box. No bruised fruit. All right, move along now. Go to work first thing in the morning. (*The iron fence is pulled up. The bookkeeper and the guard move off. Ma leads Rose of Sharon and the children away. Tom, Pa, Uncle John and Al move forward.*)

TOM. Pa, I'm a-gonna walk out an' see what all that fuss is outside the gate. Wanta come?

PA. No. I like to have a little while to jus' work an' not think about nothin'.

TOM. How 'bout you, Al?

AL. Guess I'd look aroun' in here, first.

TOM. Well, I know Uncle John won't come. Guess I'll go her alone. Got me all curious.

PA. I'd get a hell of a lot curiouser 'fore I'll do anything about it — with all them cops out there.

TOM. Maybe they ain't there now.

PA. Well, I ain't gonna find out. An' you better not tell Ma where you're a-goin'. She'll jus' squirt her head off worryin'. (*Pa and Uncle John move off.*)

TOM. (*Turning to Al.*) Ain't you curious?

AL. Guess I'll jes' look aroun' this here camp.

TOM. Lookin' for girls, huh?

AL. Mindin' my own business.

TOM. I'm still a-goin'. (*Al moves off. It grows dark. Tom moves cautiously. Dogs bark. Suddenly, out of the dark, a flashlight plays on Tom's face.*)

HOOPER RANCH GUARD. Hello — who is it? *(The guard moves a few steps closer.)*
TOM. *(Frozen.)* Who are you?
HOOPER RANCH GUARD. Where you think you're going?
TOM. Well, I thought I'd take a walk. Any law against it?
HOOPER RANCH GUARD. You better walk some other way.
TOM. Can't I even get out of here?
HOOPER RANCH GUARD. Not tonight you can't. Want to walk back, or shall I whistle some help an' take you?
TOM. Hell, it ain't nothin' to me. If it's gonna cause a mess, I don't give a darn. Sure, I'll go back.
HOOPER RANCH GUARD. Ya see, it's for your own good. Them crazy pickets might get you.
TOM. What pickets?
HOOPER RANCH GUARD. Them goddamn reds!
TOM. Oh. I didn't know 'bout them.
HOOPER RANCH GUARD. You seen 'em when you come, didn' you?
TOM. Well, I seen a bunch a guys, but they was so many cops I didn't know. Thought it was a accident.
HOOPER RANCH GUARD. Well, you better git along back.
TOM. That's OK with me, mister. *(Tom moves slowly in the hard beam of the flashlight. A song wells up out of the dark as Tom moves.)*
MAN WITH GUITAR. *(Singing.)*
> In the souls of the people,
> The grapes of wrath are filling,
> And growing heavy, growing heavy
> For the vintage...

(The flashlight snaps off. The sound of the crickets fills the night air. Tom crawls along the ground in the dark and then comes upon a group of men huddled in the shadows. The stars cut dimly through the night sky. One man with a lantern is standing guard.)
TOM. Evenin'.
CAMP GUARD. Who are you?
TOM. I guess — I'm jus' goin' past.
CAMP GUARD. Know anybody here?
TOM. No. I tell you I was jus' goin' past. *(Suddenly a camp-*

fire lights some distance away revealing another group of men and the outline of a tent. One of the group stands and looks over at Tom. It is Casy.)
CASY.   What's the matter?
TOM.   Casy! Casy! For Chris' sake, what you doin' here?
CASY.   Why, my God, it's Tom Joad! Tommy!
CAMP GUARD.   Know him, do ya? *(Casy rushes over to Tom.)*
CASY.   Know him? Christ, yes. Knowed him for years. I come west with him. Come on over here, Tom. *(Casy brings Tom near the fire. A dark-faced scowling man holds out his hand. Another older man sits near the fire.)*
FIRST MAN.   Glad to meet ya. I heard what Casy said. This the fella you was tellin' about?
CASY.   Sure. This is him. Well, for God's sake! Where's your folks?   What you doin' here?
TOM.   Well, we heard they was work this-a-way. An' we come, an' a bunch a State cops run us into this here ranch. I seen a bunch a fellas yellin'. They wouldn' tell me nothin', so I come out here to see what's goin' on. How'n hell'd you get here Casy? *(Casy and Tom sit down at the fire.)*
CASY.   Jailhouse is a kinda funny place. Here's me, been a-goin' into the wilderness to try to find out somepin'. Almost got her sometimes, too. But it's in the jail house I really got her. Some a them fellas in the tank was drunks, but mostly they was there 'cause they stole stuff; an' mostly it was stuff they needed an' couldn' get no other way. Ya see?
TOM.   No.
CASY.   Well, they was nice fellas, ya see. What made 'em bad was they need stuff. An' I begin to see, then. It's need that makes all the trouble. I ain't got it worked out. Well, one day they give us some beans that was sour. One fella started yellin', an' nothin' happened. He yelled his head off. Trusty come along an' looked in an' went on. Then another fella yelled. Well, sir, then we all got yellin'. And we all got on the same tone, an' I tell ya, it jus' seemed like that tank bulged an' give an' swelled up. By God! Then somepin' happened! They come a-runnin', an' they give us some other stuff to eat — give it to us. Ya see?

TOM. No.

CASY. Maybe I can't tell you. Maybe you got to find out. Where's your cap?

TOM. I come out without it.

CASY. How's your sister?

TOM. Hell, she's big as a cow. I bet she got twins. You ain' tol' me what's goin' on.

SECOND MAN. We struck. This here's a strike.

TOM. Well, fi' cents a box ain't much, but a fella can eat.

SECOND MAN. Fi' cents? Fi' cents? They payin' you fi' cents?

TOM. Sure. *(A heavy silence falls. Casy stares out into the dark night, his face bright in the fire light.)*

CASY. Look, Tom. We come to work there. They says it's gonna be fi' cents. They was a hell of a lot of us. We got there an' they says they're payin' two an' a half cents. A fella can't eat on that, an' if he got kids — so we says we won't take it. So they druv us off. An' all the cops in the worl' come down on us. Now they're payin' you five. When they bust this here strike — ya think they'll pay five?

TOM. I dunno. Payin' five now.

CASY. Look. We tried to camp together, an' they druv us like pigs. Scattered us. Beat the hell outa fellas. Druv us like pigs. They run you in like pigs, too. We can't las much longer. Some people ain't et for two days. You goin' back tonight?

TOM. Aim to.

CASY. Well — tell the folks in there how it is, Tom. Tell 'em they're starvin' us an' stabbin' theirself in the back. 'Cause sure as cowflops she'll drop to two an' a half jus' as soon as they clear us out.

TOM. I'll tell 'em. I don' know how. Never seen so many guys with guns. Don' know if they'll even let a fella talk.

CASY. Try an' tell 'em, Tom. They'll get two an' a half, jus' the minute we're gone. You know what two an' a half is — that's one ton of peaches picked an' carried for a dollar.

SECOND MAN. You can't do it Tom.

CASY. No — you can't do it. You can't get your food for that. Can't eat for that. *(He drops his head.)*

74

TOM. I'll try to get to tell the folks.

CASY. Look, Tom. Try an' get the folks in there to come on out. They can do it in a couple days. Them peaches is ripe. Tell 'em.

TOM. They won't.

CASY. But jus' the minute they ain't strikebreakin' they won't get no five.

TOM. I don't think they'll swalla that.

CASY. Well, tell 'em anyways.

TOM. Pa wouldn' do it. I know 'im. He'd say it wasn't none of his business.

CASY. Yes. I guess that's right. Have to take a beatin' fore he'll know.

TOM. Think Pa's gonna give up his meat on account of other fellas? An' Rosasharn oughta get milk. Think Ma's gonna wanta starve that baby jus' 'cause a bunch of fellas is yellin' outside a gate?

CASY. I wisht they could see it.

TOM. *(Exploding.)* Talkin'! Always talkin'! *(The other men freeze and listen. Tom calms himself.)* Take my brother Al. He's out lookin' for a girl. He don' care 'bout nothin' else. Couple days he'll get him a girl. Think about it all day an' do it all night. He don't give a damn.

CASY. Sure. Sure. He's jus' doin' what he's got to do. All of us like that. *(The man standing guard approaches.)*

CAMP GUARD. Goddamn it, I don't like it. *(The men put out the fire and separate, straining to hear.)*

CASY. What's the matter?

CAMP GUARD. I don' know. I jus' itch all over. Nervous as a cat.

CASY. Well, what's the matter?

CAMP GUARD. I don't know. Seems like I hear somepin', an' then I listen an' they ain't nothin' to hear.

SECOND MAN. You're jus' jumpy. They's a cloud a-sailin' over. Bet she's got thunder. That's what's itchin' him — 'lectricity.

CASY. *(Softly.)* All of 'em itchy. Them cops been sayin' how they're gonna beat the hell outa us an' run us outa the county. They figger I'm a leader 'cause I talk so much.

SECOND MAN. Wait a minute. Listen!

CASY. What is it?

SECOND MAN. I dunno.

CASY. Can't really tell if you hear it. Fools you. Get nervous. We're all nervous. Can't really tell. You hear it, Tom?

TOM. I hear it. Yeah, I hear it. I think they's guys comin' from ever' which way. We better get outa here.

SECOND MAN. *(Whispering.)* Under the bridge span — out that way. Hate to leave my tent.

CASY. Le's go. *(The men begin to scatter. Suddenly, dozens of flashlight beams slice through the dark. White luminous blades slash moving figures and human voices bark and growl and whisper from the shadows. Suddenly, Tom's face is frozen in a sword point of light.)*

FIRST MAN WITH CLUB. There they are!

SECOND MAN WITH CLUB. Stand where you are. *(One of the flashlight beams finds Casy.)*

FIRST MAN WITH CLUB. That's him. That shiny bastard. That's him. *(Casy stares blindly at the light. More lights move to Casy. Some flashlights stay pointed at Tom. Casy breathes heavily.)*

CASY. *(Moving toward the first man.)* Listen. You fellas don' know what you're doin'. You're helpin' to starve kids. *(The first man, short and heavy, steps into the light. He carries a pick handle.)*

FIRST MAN WITH CLUB. Shut up, you red son-of-a-bitch.

CASY. You don' know what you're a-doin'. *(The first man swings with the pick handle. Casy dodges down into the swing. The heavy club crashes into the side of his head with a dull crunch of bone and Casy falls sideways out of the light. The second man dashes over and shines his light on Casy's face. The preacher's eyes are wide. His mouth is open in surprise as if drawing in air. Suddenly, blood gurgles up and spills onto his chin.)*

SECOND MAN WITH CLUB. Jesus, George. I think you killed him.

FIRST MAN WITH CLUB. Serve the son-of-a-bitch right. *(Tom is frozen in horror, looking down at Casy. A bellow of rage escapes from him as he leaps at the first man and throws him to the ground. The second man rushes in, but Tom wrenches his pick handle away, swings wildly and begins beating the fallen first man about the head*

*and shoulders. The second man fumbles in the dark, grabs up a club
and rushes for Tom with a glancing blow to his head. Tom staggers
out of the cross-hatching of flashlight beams and disappears in the
shadows. The other men dash about searching and calling. Many run
off. Two or three beams of light remain in the foreground shining out.)*
HOOPER RANCH GUARD. Who's there? *(The light beams snap
off. The jaw harp thrums a rapid heartbeat in the aftermath of the
fight. Light reveals Ma near a wooden bench leaning over a bundle.
Tom crawls to the circle of light. One side of his face is caked with
blood.)*
MA. Tom, what's the matter?
TOM. Sh! Don't talk loud. I got in a fight. *(He stumbles closer
to Ma.)*
MA. Tom!
TOM. I couldn' help it, Ma.
MA. You in trouble?
TOM. Yeah. In trouble. I can't go out to work. I got to hide.
(Tom sits on the bench.)
MA. Is it bad?
TOM. Nose busted.
MA. I mean the trouble.
TOM. Yeah, bad! I went out to see what all the yellin' was
about. An' I come on Casy.
MA. The preacher?
TOM. Yeah. The preacher, on'y he was a-leadin' the strike.
They come for him.
MA. Who come for him?
TOM. I dunno. Had pick handles. They killed 'im. Busted his
head. I was standin' there. I went nuts. Grabbed the pick
handle. I — I clubbed a guy.
MA. Kill 'im?
TOM. I — dunno. I was nuts. Tried to.
MA. Was you saw?
TOM. I guess so. They had the lights on us.
MA. Tom, you got to go away.
TOM. I know, Ma.
MA. You gonna have a bad scar, Tom. An' your nose is all
crooked.

TOM. Maybe tha's a good thing. Nobody wouldn't know me, maybe. If my prints wasn't on record, I'd be glad.

MA. I want you should go a long ways off.

TOM. Hm-m. Lookie, Ma. I been all night hidin' alone. I been thinkin' about Casy. He talked a lot. Use' ta bother me. But now I been thinkin' what he said, an' I can remember — all of it.

MA. He was a good man. *(A dog barks in the distance.)* Hush — listen.

TOM. On'y the wind, Ma. I know the wind. *(Ma sits next to Tom.)*

MA. Tom, what you aimin' to do?

TOM. What Casy done.

MA. But they killed him!

TOM. Yeah. He didn' duck quick enough. He wasn' doing nothin' against the law, Ma. I been thinkin' a hell of a lot, thinkin' about our people livin' like pigs, an' the good rich lan' layin' fallow, or maybe one fella with a million acres, while a hundred thousan' good farmers is starvin'. An' I been wonderin' if all our folks got together an' yelled, like them fellas yelled, only a few of 'em outside the gate —

MA. Tom, they'll drive you, an' cut you down.

TOM. They gonna drive me anyways. They drivin' all our people.

MA. How'm I gonna know 'bout you? They might kill ya an' I wouldn' know. They might hurt ya. How'm I gonna know?

TOM. Well, maybe like Casy says, a fella ain't got a soul of his own, but on'y a piece of a big one — an' then —

MA. Then what, Tom?

TOM. Then it don' matter. Then I'll be all aroun' in the dark. I'll be ever'where — wherever you look. Wherever they's a fight so hungry people can eat, I'll be there. Wherever they's a cop beatin' up a guy, I'll be there. An' when our folks eat the stuff they raise an' live in the houses they build — why, I'll be there. See? God, I'm talkin' like Casy.

MA. I don' un'erstan'. I don' really know.

TOM. Me neither. It's jus' stuff I been thinkin' about.

MA. Tom, later — when it's blowed over, you'll come back?

You'll find us?

TOM. Sure. Now I better go.

MA. Good-by. *(Ma takes his head in her hands and kisses him on the brow. Tom stands up and turns to leave. Ma reaches for him but when Tom turns around she pulls her hands back suddenly.)*

TOM. Good-by. *(Tom ducks and crawls away. Ma's eyes are wet and burning, but she does not cry. Darkness engulfs her, and then a dim circle of light reveals the fourth narrator, a man in overalls.)*

FOURTH NARRATOR. The boxcars, twelve of them, stood end to end on a little flat beside the stream. There were two rows of six each, the wheels removed. Up the big sliding doors slatted planks ran for cat-walks. They made good houses, water-tight and draftless, room for twenty-four families, one family in each end of each car. No windows, but the wide doors stood open. *(The rusted side of a boxcar is revealed. The trough of water is open. Pa is standing in the open doorway. Ma and Uncle John are seated nearby. The fourth narrator moves out of sight.)*

MA. It's nice. It's almost nicer than anything we had.

PA. We got nothin', now. Comin' a long time — no work, no crops. What we gonna do then? How we gonna git stuff to eat? An' I tell you Rosasharn ain't so far from due. Git so I hate to think. Go diggin' back to a ol' time to keep from thinkin'. Seems like our life's over an' done.

MA. *(Moving to Pa.)* No, it ain't. It ain't, Pa. An' that's a thing a woman knows. I noticed that. Man, he lives in a jerk — baby born an' a man dies, an' that's a jerk — gets a farm an' loses his farm, an' that's a jerk. Woman, it's all one flow, like a stream, little eddies, little waterfalls, but the river, it goes right on. Woman looks at it like that. We ain't gonna die out. People is goin' on — changin' a little, maybe, but goin' right on. *(Uncle John moves to Ma with an unlit lantern. Ma holds the lantern while John lights it.)*

UNCLE JOHN. How can you tell? What's to keep ever'thing from stoppin'; all the folks from jus' gittin' tired an' layin' down? *(Ma hands the lantern back to Uncle John, who hangs it up on the wall. Rose of Sharon, Winfield, and Ruthie are all asleep on a mattress.)*

MA. Hard to say. Ever'thing we do — seems to me is aimed

79

right at goin' on. Seems that way to me. Even gettin' hungry — even bein' sick; some die, but the rest is tougher. Jus' try to live the day, jus' the day. *(Pa looks out.)*

PA. They might be a good year nex' year, back home. *(Distant thunder rolls. Al comes in through the curtain separating the two halves of the car.)*

AL. Hullo. I thought you'd be sleepin' by now.

MA. Al, we're a talkin'. Come set here.

AL. Sure — OK. I wanta talk too. I'll hafta be goin' away pretty soon now.

MA. You can't. We need you here. Why you got to go away?

AL. Well, me an' Aggie Wainwright, we figgers to get married, an' I'm gonna git a job in a garage, an' we'll have a rent' house for a while, an' — *(They stare at him.)* Well, we are, an' they ain't nobody can stop us! *(Rain begins to fall.)*

MA. Al, we're glad! We're awful glad.

AL. You are?

MA. Why, 'course we are, you're a growed man. You need a wife. Just don' go right now.

AL. I promised Aggie. We got to go. We can't stan' this no more.

MA. Jus' stay till spring. Jus' till spring. Won't you stay till spring?

AL. Well — *(Mrs. Wainwright appears from behind the curtain.)*

MRS. WAINWRIGHT. You heard yet?

MA. Yeah! Jus' heard, Mrs. Wainwright, jus' heard.

MRS. WAINWRIGHT. Oh, my! I wisht — I wisht we had a cake. I wisht we had — a cake or somepin'.

MA. I'll set on some coffee an' make up some pancakes. We got sirup.

MRS. WAINWRIGHT. Oh, my! Why — well. Look, I'll bring some sugar. We'll put sugar in them pancakes. *(She goes behind the curtain. Rose of Sharon sits up and steadies herself.)*

ROSE OF SHARON. What's a matter?

MA. Why, it's news! We're gonna have a little party 'count a Al an' Aggie Wainwright is gonna get married. *(Rose of Sharon sits perfectly still. She looks at Al. Mrs. Wainwright calls from the other end of the car.)*

MRS. WAINWRIGHT. I'm putting' a fresh dress on Aggie. I'll be right over. *(Rose of Sharon turns away slowly. A crack of thunder. Lightning flashes. Pa and Uncle John step out of the car into the rain and run down to the churning stream. Al brings Mr. Wainwright out of the boxcar and down to Pa.)*
PA. How's it look to you, John?
UNCLE JOHN. Seems to me if that crick keeps comin', she'll flood us.
PA. If we was all to get our shovels an' throw up a bank, I bet we could keep her out.
UNCLE JOHN. Yeah. Might. Dunno if them other fellas'd wanta. They'd maybe ruther move somewheres else.
PA. But these here cars is dry. Couldn' find no dry place as good as this.
UNCLE JOHN. Comin' up fast. I think we oughta go talk to the other fellas. See if they'll help ditch up. Got to git outa here if they won't. *(The men and run off. Thunder and lightning rip the air. Rose of Sharon suddenly lets out a quick sharp cry from the corner of the car. The cry is cut off. Ma whirls and goes to her. The girl is holding her breath; her eyes are filled with terror.)*
MA. What is it? *(Rose of Sharon lets out her breath and catches it again. Ma puts her hand under the covers.)* Mis' Wainwright. Oh, Mis' Wainwright! *(Mrs. Wainwright appears.)*
MRS. WAINWRIGHT. Want me?
MA. Look! It's come. It's early. *(Mrs. Wainwright bends over the girl.)*
MRS. WAINWRIGHT. Did it kinda grab you all over — quick? Open up an' answer me. *(Thunder and lightning. Rose of Sharon nods weakly. Mrs. Wainwright turns to Ma.)* Yep. It's come. Early, ya say?
MA. Maybe the fever brang it.
MRS. WAINWRIGHT. Well, she oughta be up on her feet. Oughta be walkin' aroun'.
MA. She can't. She ain't got the strength.
MRS. WAINWRIGHT. Well, she oughta. I he'ped with lots. I'll git our lantern, too. *(She calls across the curtain.)* Aggie! You take care of these here little fellas.
MA. Tha's right. Ruthie! You an' Winfiel' go down with Ag-

gie. Go on now. (*Aggie appears and holds the curtain for the children. Winfield runs to Aggie. Ruthie approaches Ma.*)

RUTHIE. Why?

MA. 'Cause you got to. Rosasharn gonna have her baby.

RUTHIE. I wanna watch, Ma. Please let me.

MA. Ruthie! You git now. You git quick. (*Ruthie follows Aggie to the other side of the car. Rose of Sharon looks up from the mattress.*)

ROSE OF SHARON. Is it a-comin'?

MA. Sure. Gonna have a nice baby. You jus' got to help us. Feel like you could get up an' walk?

ROSE OF SHARON. I can try.

MA. That's a good girl. (*Pa runs on and up into the boxcar for a shovel. A group of men with shovels and lanterns gather near the stream. To Pa.*) Her time's come.

PA. Then — then we couldn' go 'f we wanted to.

MA. No.

PA. Then we got to get that bank built.

MA. You got to. (*Pa grabs a shovel and moves back out to the stream.*)

PA. (*To the men.*) We got to get the bank built. My girl got her pains.

FIRST MAN. Baby?

PA. Yeah. We can't go now.

SECOND MAN. It ain't our baby. We kin go. (*Rose of Sharon lets out a terrible scream.*)

PA. Sure. You can go. Go on. What the hell's stoppin' you? (*Thunder cracks. The women work over Rose of Sharon, and the rain drums down. Pa jumps in the water and drives his shovel into the mud. The other men do the same.*) Higher! We got to git her higher! (*Some men appear with flashlights and sandbags. Pa watches Uncle John plunge on.*) John, take it easy. You'll kill yaself. (*Rose of Sharon screams over the thunder. The men begin to pile sandbags along the bank of the stream.*)

UNCLE JOHN. I can't he'p it. I can't stan' that yellin'. It's like — it's like when —

PA. I know. But jus' take it easy.

UNCLE JOHN. I'll run away. By God, I got to work or I'll

run away.

PA. How's she stan'?

FIRST MAN. Comin' up.

PA. She'll come up slower now. Got to flood purty far on the other side.

SECOND MAN. She's comin' up, though. *(Rose of Sharon screams repeatedly. The men work. The rain streams down. Then the screaming stops. Pa listens.)*

PA. *(To Uncle John.)* Ma'd call me if it was bore. *(A terrific crack and a flash of lightning. A ripping crash tears the air. It is the sound of a great cottonwood toppling. The men stop to look out, their mouths open. They watch the great tree split and thunder into the boiling stream.)*

UNCLE JOHN. Cottonwood.

THIRD MAN. Mighty big one.

PA. Look at 'er sink.

SECOND MAN. There goes the bank. *(The men freeze, then break and run. Uncle John slips into the water. The current swirls about his chest.)*

PA. *(Calling.)* Hey, John! What's the matter? *(He pulls Uncle John up out of the current.)*

UNCLE JOHN. Legs give out. Jus' give out.

PA. Think ya can make it awright?

UNCLE JOHN. I'll be awright. Jus' go on. *(Pa and Mr. Wainwright move up to the boxcar. Mr. Wainwright slips behind the curtain. Pa stands in the open door. Al and the other men disappear.)*

PA. How is she? *(Ma does not look up.)*

MA. Awright, I think. Sleepin'. *(Mrs. Wainwright moves to Pa. She pulls him by the elbow to the corner of the car, picks up a lantern and holds it over an apple box. Distant thunder. Curled on a newspaper is a blue shriveled little mummy. Uncle John moves up into the boxcar.)*

MRS. WAINWRIGHT. *(Softly.)* Never breathed. Never was alive. *(Uncle John turns and sits down. The rain swishes softly. Uncle John sniffles in the dark.)*

PA. We — done — what we could.

MA. *(Still not looking up.)* I know.

PA. We worked all night. An' a tree cut out the bank.

MA. I know. I heard it.

PA. Think she's gonna be all right?

MA. I dunno.

PA. Well — couldn't we — of did nothin'? *(Ma's lips are stiff and white.)*

MA. No. They was on'y one thing to do — ever — an' we done it. *(Al runs into the car soaking wet.)*

AL. I went to the truck. No use. The motor was full a water. Bat'ry foul by now. *(Ruthie comes out from behind the curtain, looks blindly at the lamp for a moment and then turns to Ma.)*

RUTHIE. Is it bore? Is the baby out? Where's the baby? *(Mrs. Wainwright picks up a sack and spreads it over the apple box in the corner. Ma moves to Ruthie kneels and embraces her.)*

MA. They ain't no baby. They never was no baby. We was wrong.

RUTHIE. Shucks! I wisht it had a been a baby. *(Uncle John and Ma help Ruthie back into the other side of the boxcar.)*

MRS. WAINWRIGHT. *(Pointing to the apple box.)* We ain't gonna git out soon. That ain't doin' no good. Jus' cause trouble an' sorra. Couldn' you fellas kinda — take it out an' bury it?

PA. Guess you're right. Jus' cause sorra. 'Gainst the law to bury it.

MRS. WAINWRIGHT. They's lots a things 'gainst the law that we can't he'p doin'. *(Mrs. Wainwright offers the box to Pa.)*

PA. Yeah. *(He turns to Uncle John.)* John, will you take an' bury it?

UNCLE JOHN. Sure. I'll do it. Sure, I will. Come on, give it to me. Come on! Give it to me! *(Mrs. Wainwright brings Uncle John the apple box.)*

PA. Shovel's standin' right behin' you. *(Uncle John takes the shovel and slips out the door. Thunder. He comes down to the trough of water and puts his shovel down. Holding the box in front of him, he edges into the swift stream. Thunder. For a time he stands watching the water swirl by, leaving its yellow foam among the willow stems. He holds the apple box against his chest. And then he leans over and sets the box in the stream and steadies it with his hand.)*

UNCLE JOHN. *(Fiercely.)* Go down an' tell 'em. Go down in the street an' rot an' tell 'em that way. That's the way you can talk. Don' even know if you was a boy or a girl. Ain't gonna find out. Go on down now, an' lay in the street. Maybe they'll know then. *(He guides the box gently out into the current and lets it go, then grabs the shovel and returns to the boxcar. The rain is now a gentle drizzle. Al pushes the curtain aside and moves into the Joad's section of the boxcar holding a dim lantern light. Ma and Rose of Sharon, soaking wet, huddle together. Pa and Uncle John, also drenched and raw, are squatting nearby. Rose of Sharon reaches up and whispers in Ma's ear. Ma nods her head.)*
MA. Yes. It's time for it. We're a-gettin' outa here. Gettin' to higher groun'. *(To Pa.)* An' you're comin' or you ain't comin', but I'm takin' Rosasharn an' the little fellas outa here.
PA. We can't!
MA. We're a-goin'.
PA. Awright, we'll go.
AL. Ma, I ain't goin'.
MA. Why not?
AL. Well — Aggie — why, her an' me — *(Ma smiles. Ruthie and Winfield appear from behind the curtain. They too are drenched.)*
MA. 'Course. You stay here, Al. Take care of the stuff. When the water goes down — why, we'll come back. Come quick, 'fore it rains harder. Come on, Rosasharn. We're goin' to a dry place.
ROSE OF SHARON. *(Weakly.)* I can walk. *(Pa and Ma help Rose of Sharon out the door. Uncle John carries Ruthie. Winfield huddles at Ma's side. Al and Aggie stand in the open door and watch the Joads move out into the rain.)*
MA. Winfiel', hang on. Al — we'll come back soon's the water's down. Al — if — if Tom comes — tell him we'll be back. Tell him to be careful. Grab on to me now, Winfiel'! *(Rain blows in billowing sheets over the trough of water. Uncle John, Ruthie, Winfield, Ma, Rose of Sharon and Pa move down to the edge of the stream and stare ahead through the curtains of rain. Al, Aggie and the boxcar are gone.)* We got to git along. Rosasharn, you feel like you could walk?

ROSE OF SHARON. Kinda dizzy. Feel like I been beat.

PA. Now we're a-goin', where' we goin'?

MA. I dunno. Come on, give your han' to Rosasharn. *(Thunder. Rose of Sharon slips. Pa and Ma pull her up.)* Pa, can you carry her? *(Pa picks up Rose of Sharon. It grows darker and the rain blows. The Joads turn slowly around. In the distance is an expanse of wooden wall.)*

PA. You ain't said where-at we're a-hurryin' to. *(Ma searches the land and flooded fields. She spots the wall far off.)*

MA. Look! Look there! I bet it's dry in that barn. Le's go there till the rain stops.

PA. Prob'ly get run out by the fella owns it. *(The Joads move up into the shadows toward the wooden wall.)*

MA. Hurry up. They's a big rain a'comin. Come on, now! Bear on, Rosasharn. *(Thunder.)* Maybe they's hay inside. *(In the dark thunder rumbles again and dies away. The rain subsides. A long verticle crack of light splits the wall of darkness and as the great barn doors open, the Joads turn facing front. Ma and Uncle John have pushed open the doors. The family stands in silhouette against the cold grey sky. Gradually, feeble shafts of light stream into the huge empty barn. A rafter is hung above with a long fringe of hay. The Joads move in slowly. Pa sets Rose of Sharon gently down near the door. Uncle John keeps the children close. Ma moves to Rose of Sharon.)* They is hay. Come on in, you. Lay down, Rosasharn. Lay down an' res'. I'll try to figger some way to dry you off.

WINFIELD. Ma! Ma!

MA. What is it? What you want?

WINFIELD. *(Pointing.)* Look! Over there. *(Ma looks. There are two figures in the gloom. A man sprawled on a blanket and a boy, his son, sitting beside him. The boy gets up slowly and turns to the Joads.)*

BOY. You own this here?

MA. No. Jus' come in outa the wet. We got a sick girl. You got a dry blanket we could use an' get her wet clothes off? *(The boy picks up a dirty comfort and holds it out to Ma.)* Thank ya. What's the matter'th that fella?

BOY. Fust he was sick — but now he's starvin'.

MA. What?

BOY. Starvin'. Got sick in the cotton. He ain't et for six days. *(Ma looks down at the man.)*

MA. Your pa?

BOY. Yeah. Says he wasn't hungry, or he jus' et. Give me the food. Now he's too weak. Can't hardly move. *(The man moves his lips. Ma kneels beside him and puts her ear close. His lips move again.)*

MA. Sure. You jus' be easy. He'll be awright. You jus' wait'll I get them wet clo'es off'n my girl. Now slip 'em off. *(Ma moves to Rose of Sharon and holds up the comfort. The girl undresses.)*

BOY. I didn' know. He said he et, or he wasn't hungry. Las' night I went an' bust a winda an' stoled some bread. Made 'im chew 'er down. But he puked it all up, an' then he was weaker. Got to have soup or milk. You folks got money to git milk?

MA. Hush. Don' worry. We'll figger somepin' out.

BOY. He's dyin', I tell you! He's starvin' to death, I tell you.

MA. Hush. *(Ma looks at Pa and Uncle John. She turns to Rose of Sharon now wrapped in the comfort. The two women look deep into each other. The girl's eyes widen.)*

ROSE OF SHARON. Yes.

MA. I knowed you would. I knowed!

ROSE OF SHARON. *(Whispering.)* Will — will you all go out? *(Ma brushes the hair from her daughter's eyes and kisses her on the forehead.)*

MA. Come on, you fellas. You come out in the shed. *(The boy opens his mouth to speak.)* Hush. Hush and git. *(Ma helps the boy up and leads him to the open door. Uncle John, Pa and the children leave. The boy looks back after his father and then goes out. Ma stands in the door for a few moments, looking back at Rose of Sharon, and then goes. Rose of Sharon stands still in the whispering barn. Then she draws the comfort about her and moves slowly to the man and stands looking down at the wasted face, into the wide frightened eyes. She slowly kneels down beside him, loosens one side of the blanket and bares her breast. He shakes his head feebly from side to side.)*

ROSE OF SHARON. You got to. *(She bends low. Her hand moves behind his head and pulls him up gently.)* There. *(Her eyes gleam.)*

There. *(A violin plays in the distance. As the lights fade slowly, Rose of Sharon looks up and across the barn. Her lips come together and smile mysteriously.)*

CURTAIN

The Grapes of Wrath

Production Notes
June 21, 1990

Here are the various lists and plots to assist in producing *The Grapes of Wrath*. They are presented here in an effort to represent what was done in the Broadway production, not as the definition of the only way to do a "correct" production. As the author's note indicates the life of the play doesn't depend upon technical wizardry. Having said that, the following lists are a fairly complete rendition of the New York production. For that production, the show was divided into rehearsal scenes, which are defined in the "Scene Explanations" list. The scene titles are also used to divide up all the other plots and lists.

APPENDIX A

SCENE EXPLANATIONS
The Grapes of Wrath

APPENDIX B

PROP PLOT (BY SCENE)

Note that this is a list of props used in each scene of the play, not a prop shift plot.

The Grapes of Wrath
PROP LIST

ACT I

OPENING MUSIC AND TOM AND CASY MEET

<u>Preset Onstage</u>
Fence
Wooden crate (for seat)
Musical saw

<u>During Scene</u>
From S.R.: 1/2 pint of "factory liquor" (Tom)
From S.L.: violin bow (saw player)
Chewing tobacco (Casy)
Harmonica (Casy)

MULEY

<u>Set Onstage</u>
Fence shifted
Broken chair
Piece of newspaper
Old shoe
Candle in holder
Wooden crate (as doorstep)
Porch post
Wooden seat crate by fire
6 fireproofed sticks for fire

During Scene
From S.L.: 2 box of matches (Tom & Casy)
Bag of belongings (Muley)
Flashlight (Willy)

CAR SALESMEN SONG

During Scene
From S.L.: cigar (Car Salesman)
Comb (Car Salesman)

Set Onstage for Uncle John's House
(During Car Salesman Song)
Truck
    w/hammer (Pa)
    w/tent tarp
    w/tool box
        with miscellaneous tools
            large wrench
            pocket knife
    w/pink curtain
    w/piece of cardboard
Ma's round backed wooden chair
Long table crate
    set on 2 base crates
    w/corn planter on top
    w/green bowl on top
Milkcan and 3 seat crates set around long table crate
Short table crate
3 seat crates set around short table crate
Straight backed wooden chair
2 pots with pork and cleaver
2 short shovels
2 tent poles
2 tall peach baskets
    w/blue blanket inside
Crate in which to pack clothes
Crate in which to pack household items

Washboard
2 lanterns
2 burlap sacks full of household items
2 kegs to store pork
Can of salt
6 fireproofed sticks to build fire

UNCLE JOHN'S HOUSE

<u>During Scene</u>

From S.L.:   nails (Pa)
                       lantern (Uncle John)
                       bag of belongings (Muley)

From S.R.:   horse collar (Noah)
                       ox pole (Noah)
                       pick ax (Noah)
                       grain scoop (Noah)
                       long handled shovel (Uncle John)
                       coil of rope (Uncle John)
                       carpetbag (Connie)

From U.S.R.:   (Inside Uncle John's House)
                       large brown checkered rag (Ma)
                       flowered tablecloth (Ma)
                       11 plates
                       11 forks
                       rag (Granma)
                       cast iron skillet w/10 biscuits and potholder
                           rag (Ma)
                       cast iron pot w/meat, potholder rag &
                           serving spoon (Ma)
                       oven rack with loaf of bread (Ma)
                       big washtub w/water in it, food holder and
                           rag (Connie)
                       lantern (Rose of Sharon)
                       fireproofed tin box w/fireproofed cards &
                         photos, gold earrings, and coin purse
                         (Ma)

Bible (Ma)
string bag w/soothing syrup, onion, salt &
    pepper shakers, wooden spoon, and 5
    assorted rags (Ma)
single mattress (Ruthie)
rolled and tied double mattress (Winfield)
crate with mason jars (Tom)
kitchen drawer with mason jar and kitchen
    items (Tom)
rag doll (Ruthie)
canteen (Uncle John)
quilt (Connie)
big blue coffee pot (Casy)
red jug (Casy)
potato pot with 7 potatoes and potato
    peeler (Uncle John)
large grey washbasin (Uncle John)
metal bucket with rag (Uncle John)
pile of clothes (Rose of Sharon)

Packed on Truck During Scene
(From Items Listed Above)
Single mattress
Rolled and tied double mattress
Ma's round backed wooden chair
4 lanterns
Small seat crate
Mason jar crate
Kitchen drawer with mason jar and kitchen items
Rag doll
Canteen
Quilt
Big blue coffee pot
Red jug
Potato pot with 7 potatoes and potato peeler
Large grey washbasin
Metal bucket with rag
Long handled shovel

Coil of rope
Carpetbag
Flowered tablecloth
Bible
String bag w/coin purse w/earrings, onion, salt & pepper
    shakers, wooden spoon, and 5 assorted rags
Pork pot
2 short shovels
2 tent poles
2 tall peach baskets
    w/blue blanket inside
Crate packed with clothes
Crate packed with household items
Washboard
2 burlap sacks full of household items
2 kegs with pork and cleaver inside
Can of salt

GRAMPA'S FUNERAL

<u>Set Onstage</u>
The Truck
2 sticks for Winfield to make cross

<u>During Scene</u>
From S.R.:   Grampa's corpse wrapped in a quilt
                cooking tripod with pot and rag
                string for Winfield to make cross
                lantern (Ma)

From S.L.:   stubby pencil (Casy)

From off truck: 3 shovels
                    4 lanterns
                    potato pot w/potatoes & potato peeler
                    small seat crate
                    Bible
                    Mason jar
                    single mattress

PROPRIETOR SCENE

<u>Set Onstage</u>

From S.R.:   5 tents on rope across stage
green basin with rag (Ma)
old wooden toolbox (camper)
2 bundles (campers)
carpetbag (camper)
whittling stick and knife (camper)
suitcase (camper)
3 lanterns (camp families)
rectangular wooden stool (Man with guitar)
baby in blanket (camp woman)

From S.L.:   rocking chair (Proprietor)
porch post with lantern
crate w/jar of silverware, rag, & cup
    (Proprietor's wife)
double mattress (camp family)
bucket of water (Uncle John)
rusty bucket (camper)
3 bundles (campers)
2 carpetbags (campers)
quilt (camp boy)
4 lanterns (camp families)
handbills (Pa and campers)

From off truck: tent tarp
2 tent poles
small seat crate

THE ROAD TO THE COLORADO RIVER

<u>Set Onstage</u>
The Truck

<u>During Scene</u>
From S.R.:   gas can (gas station attendant)
coin to pay attendants (Tom)
From S.L.:   rag (gas station attendant)

AT THE COLORADO RIVER

<u>Set Onstage</u>
The Truck

<u>During Scene</u>
From S.L.:   feed sack with shirt in it (Narrator at River)
From off truck: tin bucket
                       pink curtain to cover Granma
                       piece of cardboard
                       small seat crate
                       canteen
                       tool box

THE ROAD TO CALIFORNIA

<u>Set Onstage</u>
The Truck

<u>During Scene</u>
Notebook with pencil (agricultural inspector #1)
Flashlight (agricultural inspector #2)

INTERMISSION

<u>Set Onstage</u>
3 clotheslines
Floyd's car
Floyd's wooden stool
Dented bucket with water, frying pans, rope, quilt bundle
    (Mayor)
Baby blanket, shovel
Dirty blanket, cup, brown quilt
Green bundle, blue quilt
Blue blanket
Orange blanket, walking stick
Suitcase, pink blanket, blue blanket
Quilt, 2 pieces of newspaper, sack of belongings, purse,
    sandals

Set in S.L. Wing (From Truck)
Single mattress
Ma's round backed wooden chair
Potato pot (add water)
Small seat crate
Ma's string bag (add plate with paring knife)
Tool box

Also Set in S.L. Wing
Cooking tripod and rag

ACT II

HOOVERVILLE

During Scene
JOAD'S CAMP: single mattress
     From S.L.:   Ma's round backed wooden chair
                       potato pot with water and potatoes in it
                       plate
                       potato peeler
                       paring knife
                       wooden seat crate
                       string bag (Ma) with onion, salt &
                            pepper shakers, wooden spoon,
                            and 5 assorted rags
                       tool box with big wrench
                       cooking tripod with pot and rag
                       carpetbag (Connie's)
     From S.R.:   valve strip with valves (Floyd)
                       rag (Floyd)
                       emery paper (Floyd)
                       small seat crate (Floyd's wife)
                       baby in blanket (Floyd's wife)
                       five dollar bill (Uncle John)
                       2 one dollar coins/bills (Pa)
                       pint liquor bottle 1/4 full liquor (Uncle
                            John)
                       non-firing pistol (Officer)

firing pistol (Deputy Sheriff)
handcuffs (Officer)
pile of handbills (Contractor)
Winchester rifle (Officer)

TRANSITION FROM HOOVERVILLE TO WEEDPATCH

<u>During Transition</u>
From S.L.:   rifle (camp burner)
              3 lanterns (camp burners)
From S.R.:   red wagon of junk (Mayor of Hooverville)
              4 lanterns (camp burners)

WEEDPATCH CAMP

<u>During Scene</u>
From S.L.:   lantern (Camp Director)
              2 clipboards w/pencils (Camp Director, Head
                  of Woman's committee)
              3 white towels (Camp committee woman)
              1 white blanket (Camp committee woman)
              2 rolls of toilet paper (Camp committee woman)
              soap box (Camp committee woman)
              cigarette (Camp Director)
              cigar box with 2 corks, 2 threaded needles, scis-
                  sors, Ma's gold earrings in coin purse (Ma)
              box of clothes (Elizabeth Sandry)
              microphone on stand (band)
              bandstand crate (for camp director to stand on)
              seat crate (for saw player)

AT THE HOOPER RANCH

<u>During Scene</u>
From S.R.:   non-firing rifle (officer)
              flashlight (Hooper Ranch Guard)
From S.L.:   working double barrelled shotgun (officer)
              notebook and pencil (bookkeeper)

CASY'S TENT IN THE STRIKE

<u>Set Onstage</u>
2 stools (Casy, Second Man)

<u>During Scene</u>
From S.R.:   lantern (Man at Camp)
                       3 flashlights (Men chasing strikers)
From S.L.:   box of matches (Casy)
                       4 large flashlights (Men chasing strikers)
                       long pickhandle (Second Man with club)
                       short pickhandle (First Man with club)

MA & TOM SAY GOODBYE

<u>Set Onstage</u>
Wooden bench
Rolled, tied mattress and quilt

BOXCAR CAMP

<u>Set Onstage</u>
Weighted apple box
      with cloth to wrap dead baby
Single mattress
Quilt
Dirty blanket w/pouch for dead baby
Dead baby
Small seat crate
Lantern
Ma's round backed wooden chair
Burlap sack (to cover baby)
Long handled shovel (Pa)

<u>During Scene</u>
From S.R.:   lantern (Mrs. Wainwright)
                       2 shovels (men in river)
                       2 lanterns (men in river)
                       2 buckets of warm water offstage to douse
                             Ruthie, Winfield, Aggie

wading pool offstage for dousing of Ruthie,
       Winfield, Aggie
From S.L.:   box of matches (Uncle John)
       1 shovel (men in river)
       7 sandbags (men in river)
       1 lantern (men by river)
       2 buckets of warm water offstage to douse Ma
           and Rose of Sharon
       wading pool offstage for dousing of Ma and
           Rose of Sharon

THE BARN

<u>Set Onstage</u>
Starving man's quilt (to give to Rose of Sharon)
Starving man's blanket

PERSONAL PROPS
Pa — pipe, tobacco in canister, box of matches
Casy — harmonica, chewing tobacco, box of matches

GENERAL USAGE PROPS
Small boxes of matches
Box of large kitchen matches
Toothpicks

BAND INSTRUMENTS
Man with Guitar — guitar
2nd Band Member — fiddle
3rd Band Member — harmonica, saw, jaw harp, banjo
4th Band Member — accordion, washtub bass

APPENDIX C

PROP — TOP OF SHOW PRESET (BY LOCATION)

This is a list of where the props were set at the top of the show in New York. It may be of little use, except as an indication of where things were set.

The Grapes of Wrath
PROP PRESET — TOP OF SHOW

ONSTAGE
Seat crate
Musical saw
Fence diagonally across stage
6 sticks S.R. of right fire
2 sticks D.S.R. near proscenium
6 sticks S.L. of center fire

STAGE RIGHT

Downstage Right
Porch post
Broken chair
Valve strip and valves
Dirty rag
Emery paper
Newspaper
Old shoe
Candle in holder
Crate (used as doorstep)
Ma's round backed wooden chair
Milkcan
Front end of Graham automobile

Loaded On Truck
Pa's hammer
Grey small seat crate
Brown seat crate
Long table crate
      w/corn planter inside (S.R. end)
      w/green bowl inside (S.L. end)
Short table crate
2 base crates (for table crate)
Piece of cardboard
Pink curtain
Tool box
      w/big wrench
      w/pocket knife
Orange tent tarp

Prop Shelf Unit
Tied rolled mattress and quilt
Green basin
      w/rag
Old wooden tool box
2 babies in blankets
Connie's carpetbag
4 large black flashlights
Burlap sack
Small liquor bottle
      3/4 filled with apple juice
Box of matches
      w/4 large kitchen matches
Coin
Winfield's string
Large green liquor bottle
      1/4 filled with water
Two $5 bills
Box of kitchen matches
2 small boxes of matches
Cup for hot matches
Cup of toothpicks

6 sticks
Handcuffs
Non-firing pistol
Pile of handbills
Gas can
Long blue bundle
Weighted carpetbag
Striped suitcase
Shoulder strapped beige bag
Domino bag
5 lanterns
Firing pistol

<u>S.R. General Area</u>
2 stools
Horse collar
Ox pole
Pick ax
Grain scoop
3 long handled shovels
Coil of rope
Winchester rifle
Shotgun
Bench
2 buckets to douse kids
Pool for dousing
Red wagon of junk
Cooking tripod
    w/pot and rag
Grampa's corpse wrapped in quilt
Tall crate seat
Short crate seat
Wooden straight backed chair
Keg
    w/salt can inside
Crate
    w/peach basket w/2 lanterns
    w/empty keg

Crate
>   w/dressing items
>   w/washboard
>   w/burlap sack of household items

Tents on tent rope
Single mattress
Rolled and tied double mattress
Big washtub
>   w/water in it
>   w/container for food and rag

Moveable Prop Shelf (Used U.S. of Uncle John's House)

11 forks
11 plates
Cast iron skillet
>   w/10 biscuits
>   w/serving spoon
>   w/potholder rag

Cast iron pot
>   w/chunks of pumpernickel
>   w/potholder rag

Oven rack
>   w/loaf of bread

Dish pan
Mason jar crate
Kitchen drawer
>   w/empty Mason jar
>   w/misc. dressing

Pile of clothes

ON BACK OF "UNCLE JOHN'S HOUSE" FLYING UNIT

On Shelves

Large brown rag
Flowered tablecloth
Rag (Granma)

Tin box
    w/cards and photos
    w/gold earrings
    w/coin purse
Bible
    w/blank pages
String bag
    w/soothing syrup
    w/onion
    w/salt and pepper shakers
    w/wooden spoon
    w/5 assorted rags
    rag doll
    canteen
    quilt

Hanging On Snap Hooks
Lantern
Big blue coffee pot
Red jug
Potato pot
    w/7 potatoes
    w/potato peeler
Large grey washbasin
Metal bucket
    w/rag

STAGE LEFT

General S.L. Area
Microphone
Rocking chair
2 short shovels
2 pots
    w/pork & cleaver
2 tent poles

2 tall peach baskets
     w/blue blanket
     w/burlap sack of household goods
7 lanterns
2 shovels
7 sandbags
Grey slat crate
     w/jar of silverware, rag, cup
2 stools
Child's wading pool for dousing folks
2 buckets of warm water to douse folks

<u>Prop Shelf Units</u>
4 large black flashlights
Double mattress
Weighted apple box
Dead baby
Patterned cloth to wrap baby
Boxcar quilt
Dirty blanket w/pouch
Bucket of water
3 white towels
1 white blanket
2 rolls of toilet paper
Soap box
Pile of handbills
Nails
Stubby pencil
Cigar
Comb
A few dollar bills
Silver cup
Box of toothpicks
Small boxes of matches
Box of large kitchen matches
Cup for hot matches
Pack of cigarettes
2 notebooks with pencils

Rag doll
Baby wrapped in blanket
2 clipboards w/pencils and paper
Cigar box
     w/2 corks
     w/2 threaded needles
     w/scissors
Plate
     w/paring knife
Feed sack
     w/shirt
Starving man's quilt
Starving man's blanket
Box of clothes
Rusty bucket
Green bundle w/rag
Green carpet sack
2 carpetbags
1 working shotgun
1 non-working shotgun
Long pickhandle
Short pickhandle
Walking stick
Dented bucket with water
Frying pans and rope
Red/blue quilt bundle
4 assorted quilts
4 assorted blankets

APPENDIX D

CAST BREAKDOWN & COSTUME PLOT

The New York cast had 35 actors in it, who played approximately 62 parts. Following is a cast list that enumerates how roles were cast by actor. After that is a detailed costume plot that can also be used to determine which actors were in which scene, and what they played in that scene. Almost all of the costumes were distressed to some degree and there were few vibrant colors. Many of the actors appeared barefoot in parts of the play, which is indicated in the detailed costume plot. If no footwear is indicated, the actor was barefoot in the scene. Most of the actors wore socks when they were wearing shoes, which is not always indicated in the list. One item of special concern are all the costumes that get wet in the flood scene (The Boxcar Camp). They need special attention to prevent mildew and the like. Many of the actors who actually got into the river tank during the scene wore canvas deck shoes to help with traction. Wardrobe will also need a large supply of towels for the cast.

The Grapes of Wrath need not be performed by an ensemble this large. Further doubling of roles could reduce the size of the cast to between 20 and 25 actors.

CHARACTER LIST BY ACTOR

1. Tom Joad
2. Jim Casy
3. Ma Joad
4. Pa Joad
5. Granma
6. Grampa
7. Uncle John
8. Al
9. Noah
10. Rose of Sharon

11. Connie Rivers
12. Ruthie
13. Winfield
14. First Narrator, Car Salesman #5, The Man Going Back, Weedpatch Camp Director, Mr. Wainwright, Ensemble #1.
15. Second Narrator, Elizabeth Sandry, Ensemble #2.
16. Man with Guitar
17. Man with Saw, Harmonica, Banjo, Jaw Harp.
18. Violinist.
19. Man with Accordion, Washtub Bass.
20. Mrs. Wainwright, Ensemble #3.
21. Muley Graves, Floyd Knowles, Ensemble #4.
22. The Man in the Barn's Son, Ensemble #5.
23. First Agricultural Officer, First Officer (Hooverville), First Armed Guard, First Man with Club, Ensemble #6.
24. Car Salesman #3, Ensemble #7.
25. Willy, Mayor of Hooverville, Ensemble #8.
26. Proprietor's Daughter, Woman Who Gets Shot, Aggie Wainwright, Ensemble #9.
27. Gas Station Owner, Contractor, Third Narrator, Hooper Ranch Guard, Ensemble #10.
28. Car Salesman #4, Proprietor, Second Man (Casy's Tent scene), Ensemble #11.
29. Camp Guard, The Man in the Barn, Ensemble #12.
30. Gas Station Attendant, Second Officer (Hooverville), Second Armed Guard, Ensemble #13.
31. Second Agricultural Officer, First Man, Guard with Shotgun, Ensemble #14.
32. Weedpatch Camp Nurse, Ensemble #15.
33. Car Salesman #2, Hooper Ranch Bookkeeper, Second Man with Club, Ensemble #16.
34. Car Salesman #1, Deputy Sheriff, Fourth Narrator, Ensemble #17.
35. Al's Girl, Ensemble #18.

ACT I

TOM AND CASY MEET

First Narrator — Grey herringbone pants, brown gabardine shirt, brown cotton jacket, black shoes, brown fedora, brown suspenders.

Man with Saw — Denim pants, red and yellow plaid shirt, black shoes, black wool knit vest.

Tom Joad — Cheap new prison issue suit, blue workshirt, tweed cap, brown boots, undershirt, period underwear, brown belt.

Jim Casy — Distressed summer linen two piece suit, textured vest, distressed canvas shoes, black bowler hat, distressed formal shirt, rope belt, maroon kerchief.

SONG — DUST BOWL FOLK SONG

Man with Guitar — Denim overalls, long underwear shirt, brown cowboy boots, brown felt hat.

MULEY SCENE

Tom — Same.

Casy — Same.

Muley Graves — Denim overalls, blue plaid flannel shirt, green plaid wool jacket, black boots, broken glasses.

Willy — Brown cotton pants, blue suspenders, red plaid shirt, dark brown cowboy hat, brown shoes, brown corduroy coat with plaid collar.

CAR SALESMEN SONG

Pa — Denim overalls, blue workshirt, brown boots, blue wool vest, blue suit coat, grey fedora.

Car Salesman #1 — Brown wool pants, grey suspenders, off-white cotton shirt, brown boots, light purple print tie.

Car Salesman #2 — Light brown tweed cotton pants, blue suspenders, off-white silk shirt with gold stripes, white shoes.

Car Salesman #3 — Charcoal grey wool pants, white suspenders, peach gabardine shirt, blue bow tie, black shoes with grey uppers.

Car Salesman #4 — Brown linen pants, white suspenders, light brown with brown print cotton shirt, brown print tie, brown fedora, brown and white saddle shoes, brown kerchief.

Car Salesman #5 — Black with blue tweed wool pants, grey suspenders, blue and yellow plaid gabardine shirt, black shoes, blue with grey and beige bow tie.

Man with Guitar — Same.

Man with Banjo — See Man with Saw in TOM AND CASY MEET, add denim jacket.

Violinist — Blue crepe with beige print dress, black shoes, straw hat with brown hat band.

Man with Accordion — Brown wool pants, brown suspenders, grey and brown twill shirt, brown felt hat, off-white suede shoes, brown cotton jacket.

Ens. #6 — Denim overalls, short sleeve peach gabardine shirt, brown boots, blue herringbone wool vest.

Ens. #13 — Beige cotton pants with grease stains, off-white shirt with grease stains, salt and pepper wool suit coat, black suspenders, brown boots.

Ens. #14 — Denim pants, rope belt, red plaid shirt, brown double-breasted wool vest, brown leather jacket, black boots, brown fedora.

UNCLE JOHN'S HOUSE

Tom — Same, add denim jacket during scene, take off suit coat.

Casy — Same.

Ma — Off-white with yellow plaid dress, grey apron with tear-away strip, add pink linen jacket, grey felt hat, add tan cotton stockings and brown shoes during scene.

Pa — Same.

Granma — Long black and white calico dress, flowered sun bonnet, black shoes, off-white night dress (underdressed), grey wig, crocheted rust shawl.

Grampa — Denim overalls, short sleeved off-white union suit, brown suede shoes, grey felt cowboy hat.

Uncle John — Denim pants, maroon suspenders, brown plaid flannel shirt, black wool suit coat, brown boots, brown fedora, blue kerchief, undershirt.

Al — Denim pants, brown belt, light brown cotton jacket, blue and white striped engineer's cap, light brown kerchief, undershirt, period underwear.

Noah — Denim overalls, long underwear shirt, brown cowboy boots, beige western hat.

Rose of Sharon — Off-white pique summer dress with blue roses, blue felt cloche, off-white shoes.

Connie Rivers — Grey wool pants, blue patterned suspenders, sea-green gabardine shirt, light grey fedora, brown shoes, blue cotton jacket.

Ruthie — Green checked summer cotton dress.

Winfield — Denim overalls, blue with yellow plaid shirt, golden brown suede jacket, denim cap.

Man with Guitar — Same.

Man with Banjo & Harmonica — Same.

Violinist — Same.

Man with Accordion — Same.

SONG — "66 IS THE PATH"

Tom — Same.

Casy — Same.

Ma — Same, less jacket and hat.

Pa — Same.

Granma — Same.

Uncle John — Same.

Al — Same.

Noah — Same.

Rose of Sharon — Same, add 3 month pregnant pad.

Connie — Same.

Ruthie — Same.

Winfield — Same.

Muley — Same.

Man with Guitar — Same.

Man with Banjo — Same.
Violinist — Same.
Man with Accordion — Same.

GRAMPA'S FUNERAL
Tom — Same.
Casy — Same.
Ma — Same, tear off strip on apron during scene.
Pa — Same.
Granma — Same.
Uncle John — Same.
Al — Same, add blue and white flannel shirt.
Noah — Same.
Rose of Sharon — Same.
Connie — Same.
Ruthie — Same.
Winfield — Same.

SONG — DUST BOWL HYMN
Tom — Same.
Casy — Same.
Ma — Same.
Pa — Same.
Granma — Same.
Uncle John — Same.
Al — Same.
Noah — Same.
Rose of Sharon — Same.
Connie — Same.
Ruthie — Same.
Winfield — Same.
Man with Guitar — Same.
Man with Banjo — Same.
Violinist — Same.
Man with Accordion — Same.

MA AND AL IN THE TRUCK
Ma — Same, add hat and jacket.
Al — Same.
Winfield — Same.
Ruthie — Same.
Tom — Same.
Casy — Same.
Pa — Same.
Rose of Sharon — Same.
Noah — Same.
Granma — Same.
Man with Guitar — Same.
Man with Banjo — Same.
Violinist — Same.
Man with Accordion — Same.

PROPRIETOR SCENE
Tom — Same.
Casy — Same.
Ma — Same, less hat and jacket.
Pa — Same.
Granma — Same, takes dress and bonnet off during scene.
Uncle John — Same.
Al — Same, less shirt.
Noah — Same.
Rose of Sharon — Same.
Connie — Same.
Ruthie — Same.
Winfield — Same.
The Man Going Back — Distressed brown wool suit, distressed brown checked shirt, distressed blue and white plaid shirt, t-shirt, bare feet.
Man with Guitar — Same.
Man with Banjo — Same.
Violinist — Same.
Man with Accordion — Same.
Proprietor — Denim overalls, blue workshirt, red and brown wool hunting jacket, brown checked cap, brown shoes.

Proprietor's Daughter — White with blue flowered print dress, brown and pink print apron, black shoes.

Ens. #2 — Black and orange print dress under grey with orange and yellow print short sleeve dress, orange cloche, black shoes, brown stockings.

Ens. #3 — White with brown print dress, brown felt hat, black shoes, pea-green wool jacket, light brown stockings.

Ens. #4 — Brown wool pants, maroon with grey and gold plaid shirt, dark grey suit coat, straw fedora, two-toned brown shoes.

Ens. #5 — Blue and white striped denim overalls, red and green plaid shirt, brown felt cap, black boots.

Ens. #6 — Brown wool pants, grey with light brown and blue plaid gabardine shirt, brown fedora, brown boots, blue wool herringbone vest.

Ens. #7 — Denim pants, rope belt, green suspenders, blue workshirt, brown wool vest, denim jacket with light brown corduroy collar, black boots, grey fedora.

Ens. #8 — Denim overalls, blue and brown checked shirt, light brown cowboy hat, brown shoes, denim jacket.

Ens. #10 — Beige cotton pants with grease stains, off-white cotton shirt with grease stains, beige suspenders, black felt vest, brown shoes.

Ens. #12 — Denim pants; rope belt; grey and green plaid gabardine shirt; blue, red, and yellow plaid cap; black boots.

Ens. #13 — See "CAR SALESMEN SONG," add grey fedora.

Ens. #14 — See CAR SALESMEN.

Ens. #15 — Denim overalls, grey with brown and gold plaid gabardine shirt, black felt hat, brown boots.

Ens. #16 — Black wool pants, brown suspenders, blue and black plaid shirt, grey boots, brown plaid cap.

Ens. #17 — Denim overalls, blue workshirt, black boots, denim jacket, grey fedora.

Ens. #18 — Denim pants, brown flowered silk blouse, black shoes.

THE ROAD TO THE COLORADO RIVER

Tom — Same.

Casy — Same.

Ma — Same.

Pa — Same.

Granma — Same.

Uncle John — Same.

Al — Same, less shirt.

Noah — Same.

Rose of Sharon — Same.

Connie — Same.

Ruthie — Same.

Winfield — Same.

Man with Guitar — Same.

Man with Banjo — Same.

Violinist — Same.

Man with Accordion — Same.

Second Narrator — Same as Ens. #2 in PROPRIETOR SCENE.

Gas Station Owner — Same as Ens. #10 in PROPRIETOR SCENE, less vest, add beige service station cap with grease stains.

Gas Station Attendant — Same as Ens. #13 in PROPRIETOR SCENE, less suit coat and fedora, add beige service station cap with grease stains.

Ens. #7 — Same as in PROPRIETOR SCENE.

AT THE COLORADO RIVER

Tom — Same, takes off pants, shirt, and boots during scene to get into river, then puts back on during scene.

Casy — Same.

Ma — Same.

Pa — Same.

Granma — Same.

Uncle John — Same.

Al — Same, takes off all his clothes during scene to get into river, then puts all back on during scene.

Noah — Same, gets into river wearing overalls only, then carries off all his clothes on exit.
Rose of Sharon — Same.
Connie — Same.
Ruthie — Same.
Winfield — Same.

THE ROAD TO CALIFORNIA
Tom — Same.
Casy — Same.
Ma — Same.
Pa — Same.
Granma — Same.
Uncle John — Same.
Al — Same.
Rose of Sharon — Same.
Connie — Same.
Ruthie — Same.
Winfield — Same.
First Narrator — Same as in TOM AND CASY MEET.
Man with Guitar — Same.
Man with Banjo — Same.
Violinist — Same.
Man with Accordion — Same.
First Agricultural Officer — Arizona Governmental Uniform–1938, (blue coat, blue hat, blue pants, black shoes).
Second Agricultural Officer — Arizona Governmental Uniform–1938, (blue coat, blue hat, blue pants, black shoes).

ACT II
HOOVERVILLE
Tom — Same.
Casy — Same.
Ma — Same, less shirt, add jacket and hat, take off during scene.
Pa — Same.

Uncle John — Same.

Al — Same.

Rose of Sharon — Same, carries Connie's jacket at end of scene.

Connie — Same.

Ruthie — Same.

Winfield — Denim pants, maroon suspenders, brown plaid with red shirt, golden brown suede jacket, denim cap.

Mayor of Hooverville — Blue and white striped denim overalls, distressed grey western hat.

Floyd Knowles — Grey striped wool pants, black suspenders, dark green cotton shirt, grey fedora, two-toned brown shoes.

Contractor — Beige wool pants, maroon gabardine shirt, beige cowboy hat, dark brown suit coat, brown shoes.

Deputy Sheriff — Blue wool pants, brown suspenders, peach cotton shirt, black leather jacket with badge, black fedora, brown boots, black leather gunbelt with holster and pistol.

First Officer — Charcoal grey wool pants, maroon suspenders, green with gold plaid gabardine shirt, brown leather jacket with badge, black fedora, brown boots.

Second Officer — Dark blue wool pants, grey suspenders, brown leather jacket with badge, brown boots, grey fedora.

Man with Guitar — Same.

Man with Harmonica — same as Man with Banjo in THE ROAD TO CALIFORNIA.

Violinist — Off-white with brown print dress, black shoes.

Man with Accordion — Same.

Woman Who Gets Shot — Light denim skirt, distressed blue workshirt, blue cotton jacket, grey felt hat, black shoes.

Ens. #1 — Denim overalls, green plaid flannel shirt, black shoes.

Ens. #2 — Red and beige striped dress, green plaid gabardine shirt.

Ens. #3 — Light blue cotton dress, black shoes, maroon cardigan.

Ens. #5 — Ragged denim pants, red and grey plaid short
    sleeve gabardine shirt, brown striped wool suit coat,
    brown boots.
Ens. #6 — Denim overalls, green with gold plaid shirt, brown
    boots.
Ens. #7 — Same as in THE ROAD TO THE COLORADO
    RIVER.
Ens. #10 — Denim overalls, red and blue plaid shirt, brown
    shoes.
Ens. #11 — Denim overalls, brown plaid flannel shirt over
    distressed white cotton shirt, black suit coat, brown
    shoes.
Ens. #12 — Denim pants, blue workshirt, black wool suit
    coat, black boots, grey fedora.
Ens. #13 — Denim pants, green suspenders, red and grey
    plaid gabardine shirt, grey herringbone cap, brown
    boots.
Ens. #14 — same as in PROPRIETOR SCENE.
Ens. #15 — Brown print wrap-around dress.
Ens. #16 — Black wool pants, green and brown plaid shirt,
    grey boots.
Ens. #17 — Denim overalls, blue and brown plaid flannel
    shirt, black boots.
Ens. #18 — Rust flowered skirt, green wool blouse.

WEEDPATCH CAMP
Tom — Same.
Ma — Same, less apron.
Pa — Same.
Uncle John — Same.
Al — Same, add green and red plaid flannel shirt.
Rose of Sharon — Multi-colored cotton print dress with
    patch pockets, pregnant pad at 6 months.
Ruthie — Yellow and brown print dress.
Winfield — Same.
Weedpatch Camp Director — Blue wool pants, off-white
    gabardine shirt, grey Stetson hat, silver bolo tie, wire
    rim glasses, black shoes.

Elizabeth Sandry — green and black cotton print dress.

Al's Girl — Light blue and orange print cotton dress, off-white petticoat, black shoes, red flowered apron, take off apron during scene.

Third Narrator — Denim overalls, blue and red plaid shirt, brown herringbone cap, brown shoes, grey wool vest.

Weedpatch Camp Nurse — Off-white with grey plaid dress, grey apron with red cross, black shoes, take off apron during scene.

Man with Guitar — Same.

Man with Banjo and Saw — Same.

Violinist — Beige skirt, off-white embroidered peasant shirt, brown suede shoes.

Man with Washtub Bass — Same as Man with Accordion in HOOVERVILLE.

Ens. #3 — Salmon crepe dress, brown jacket, off-white apron with pink edging, brown shoes, take off apron and jacket during scene.

Ens. #4 — Same as PROPRIETOR SCENE.

Ens. #5 — Blue and white striped denim overalls, red and grey plaid short sleeve shirt, brown cap, brown boots.

Ens. #6 — Same as First Officer in HOOVERVILLE, less jacket and black fedora, add grey fedora and grey wool vest.

Ens. #7 — Same as in HOOVERVILLE.

Ens. #8 — Brown cotton pants, bluish grey suspenders, red plaid shirt, brown shoes.

Ens. #9 — White with green print dress, brown shoes, brown and pink print apron, rose cotton jacket, take off apron and jacket during scene.

Ens. #11 — Blue cotton pants, distressed white cotton shirt, brown wool vest, brown shoes.

Ens. #12 — Same as in HOOVERVILLE, less shirt and coat, add wine plaid gabardine shirt.

Ens. #13 — Same as Second Officer in HOOVERVILLE, less jacket and fedora.

Ens. #14 — Denim pants, rope belt, green cotton shirt, brown fedora, black boots, blue wool vest.

Ens. #16 — Denim pants, pale green gabardine shirt, brown belt, brown fedora, beige cotton jacket, grey boots.

Ens. #17 — Same as Deputy Sheriff in HOOVERVILLE, less jacket and fedora.

AT THE HOOPER RANCH

Tom — Same.

Ma — Same.

Pa — Same.

Uncle John — Same.

Al — Same, less shirt.

Rose of Sharon — Same.

Ruthie — Same.

Winfield — Same.

Hooper Ranch Guard — Same as Third Narrator in WEED-PATCH, add brown leather jacket and brown fedora.

First Armed Guard — Same as Ens. #6 in WEEDPATCH, add brown leather jacket and brown fedora.

Second Armed Guard — Same as Ens. #13 in WEEDPATCH, add brown leather jacket and brown fedora.

Third Armed Guard with Shotgun — Same as Ens. #14 in WEEDPATCH, add brown and beige wool plaid jacket.

Hooper Ranch Bookkeeper — Same as Ens. #16 in WEED-PATCH.

Ens. #2 — Same.

Ens. #3 — Same.

Ens. #4 — Same.

Ens. #5 — Same.

Ens. #7 — Same.

Ens. #8 — Same.

Ens. #9 — Same.

Ens. #11 — Same.

Ens. #12 — Same.

Ens. #15 — Same.

Ens. #17 — Same.

Ens. #18 — Same.

CASY'S TENT IN THE STRIKE

Tom — Same, less hat.

Casy — Same, less formal shirt, add distressed long underwear shirt.

Camp Guard — Denim pants, green and beige plaid flannel shirt, grey fedora, denim vest with lambs wool lining, black boots.

Second Man — Denim overalls, distressed white shirt, brown vest, brown plaid cap, brown shoes.

First Man — Same as Third Armed Guard with Shotgun in HOOPER RANCH.

First Man with Club — Same as First Armed Guard in HOOPER RANCH.

Second Man with Club — Denim pants, brown belt, green and brown plaid flannel shirt, brown corduroy coat with leather collar, grey boots.

Hooper Ranch Guard — Same.

Ens. #1 — Denim overalls, green plaid shirt, black shoes, black suit coat.

Ens. #4 — Same.

Ens. #5 — Same.

Ens. #7 — Same.

Ens. #8 — Same.

Ens. #13 — Same as Second Armed Guard AT THE HOOPER RANCH.

Ens. #17 — Same as Deputy Sheriff in HOOVERVILLE.

MA AND TOM SAY GOODBYE

Tom — Same.

Ma — Same, add Al's shirt from GRAMPA'S FUNERAL SCENE.

THE BOXCAR CAMP

Ma — Same.

Pa — Distressed denim overalls, distressed blue workshirt, canvas shoes, grey fedora.

Uncle John — Same, less boots, add canvas shoes.

Rose of Sharon — Shredded blue plaid dress with brown collar, pregnant pad at 9 months, remove pad during scene.

Ruthie — Distressed green print wrap-around dress.

Winfield — Distressed denim pants, distressed rust plaid shirt.

Mrs. Wainwright — Salmon and brown print dress, maroon cardigan, black shoes.

Mr. Wainwright — Same as Ens. #1 in CASY'S TENT, less coat and shoes, add canvas shoes.

Aggie Wainwright — White with rust print dress.

Man with Guitar — Same.

Fourth Narrator — Denim overalls, blue workshirt, denim jacket, canvas shoes.

Ens. #4 — Same, less jacket and hat.

Ens. #6 — Denim overalls.

Ens. #7 — Same, less jacket.

Ens. #8 — Denim overalls, brown and blue checked shirt, light brown cowboy hat, brown shoes.

Ens. #10 — Same as Hooper Ranch Guard, less coat and hat.

Ens. #11 — Same as Second Man in CASY'S TENT.

Ens. #13 — Denim pants, green suspenders, red and grey gabardine shirt.

Ens. #14 — Denim pants, green cotton shirt.

Ens. #16 — Grey cotton pants, blue workshirt.

THE BARN

Ma — Same, less shirt.

Pa — Same.

Uncle John — Same.

Rose of Sharon — Same.

Ruthie — Same.

Winfield — Same.

Man in the Barn — Ragged blue wool pinstripe pants, shredded blue workshirt.

His Son — Shredded grey cotton shirt, ragged denim pants.

APPENDIX E

THE CAMPFIRES

THE FIRES
The fire pits were constructed by a qualified theatrical special effects consultant, and were made to meet specifications provided by the New York City Fire Department. It is important to consult your local fire department and a professional consultant before attempting any fire effects. The system in New York used propane fuel. Needless to say, all props, costumes, and scenery (including the flooring) near the fire pits were fireproofed. The handles to open the fire pits were recessed into the floor. The pits themselves were basically boxes constructed out of steel plates welded together.

The Grapes of Wrath
FIRE FX CUES

Total Use of Fires

Fire #1 — S.L.	24.5 Min.	2 Cues
Fire #2 — S.R.C.	17.75 Min.	3 Cues
Fire #3 — S.R.	21.5 Min.	2 Cues

Cue #	Fire #	Scene Name	Duration	Page #	Time into Act
			Act I		
1	2	Muley	1.75 Min.	14	10 Min.
2	3	Uncle John	3.5 Min.	26	28 Min.
3	2	Funeral	7.5 Min.	28	33 Min.
4	2	Proprietor	8.5 Min.	33	48 Min.
			Act II		
5	1 + 3	Hooverville	19.75 Min. 18.25 Min.	49	0 Min.
6	1	Casy's Tent	4.75 Min.	73	40 Min.

APPENDIX F

WATER EFFECTS

THE RIVER

The river tank is used twice in the show, first as the Colorado River in Act I, and then in the boxcar scene as the flooding stream. The tank is covered by a sliding platform on the stage apron. Additionally, the tank served to catch the water used in the rain effect. It was constructed out of black fiberglass and was molded into steps to help the actors get into it. While the fiberglass is being done, a small amount of grit should be added to aid in traction. Color can be added into the final interior coat, if desired. The recommended product for the interior surface is called Gel Coat, which is used on boats. The tank was fitted with a circulator pump, a Jacuzzi water heater, and a filter. The drain was placed on the bottom of the tank and the return about a foot below the water line. The tank was tested on a regular basis for chlorine and pII level. Test kits are readily available at a swimming pool supply company. It is recommended that the construction of the pool be subcontracted out to a company that manufactures pools or hot tubs.

THE RAIN

The rain pipes were constructed of plastic PVC pipe which were drilled and fitted with nozzles similar to those used on Hudson sprayers. There were two separate rain pipes, one providing a misty rain, and the other a downpour type rain. The nozzles lend control over the look of the rain, and aid in aiming it. The only problem that these nozzles present is that the water can drip during the final scene and bows. This can be prevented in a variety of ways, by draining all the water out of the pipes by introducing air into the system, or by rotating the rain pipe itself and pointing the nozzles up, or by closing off all the water valves and just letting the water run out. How well any of these options work will depend on the location of the water source, and the direction the supply hoses run, and the amount of water pressure. It is also important that the rain water be moderate in temperature, so the actors will not catch colds. In the New York production there was a water heater on a gallery above the stage, and hoses ran from there to the rain pipes.

APPENDIX G

THE TRUCK

The truck used in New York was actually a Ford Model A, modified and shortened. The truck had two separate drive mechanisms, one that took it stage right and left, and one that pivoted it. The motor for the pivot was mounted under the truck. No attempt was made to make the movement of the truck completely "real." The front wheels did not turn, the undercarriage and the real casters were exposed, and the truck's movement was stylized. Be aware that the truck will require a relatively flat surface on which to turn. There are a lot of people on it at times, and when it's loaded the truck is difficult to get over any hills and valleys (including rough floorboards). Also check sight lines in the theatre so that people sitting in the front seat of the truck can be seen by the whole audience. The roof of the cab may need to be raised a bit if there is a balcony. Be sure to use deep hooks on the sides of the truck to prevent things from falling off as the truck turns and moves. The headlights and taillights worked in the night scenes, and can be done either through an electrical umbilical, or by using a real car battery and keeping it charged.

TRUCK MOVEMENT

CUE #	MOVE (Pivots in Degrees)	DIRECTION	SPEED	SCENE
1	ENTER FROM S.R.- TRAVEL TO S.L.-STOP	S.R. TO S.L.	NORM	In Car Salesmen Song
2	BACK UP TO C-STOP- THEN PIVOT 90 TO FACE D.S.	L. TO R. PIVOT-CW	NORM	Near end Uncle John's house
3	PIVOT 90 TO FACE S.R.- THEN GO FWD TO S.R.	PIVOT-C.W. L. TO R.	NORM	During "66 is the Path" song
4	BACK UP TO C-STOP- THEN PIVOT 90 TO FACE D.S.	R. TO L. PIVOT- C.C.W.	NORM	During Dust Bowl Hymn
5	PIVOT 90 TO FACE S.R.- THEN EXIT INTO S.R. WING	PIVOT-C.W. L. TO R.	NORM	At top of Pro- prietor Scene
6	BACK ON FROM S.R.- STOP	R. TO L.	NORM	At end Pro- prietor Scene
7	PIVOT 90 TO FACE D.S.	PIVOT-C.W.	NORM	For Gas Station
8	PIVOT 170 TO FACE U.S. (SLIGHT DIAG.)	PIVOT-C.W.	NORM	For At the Colorado River
9	PIVOT 190 TO FACE D.S.	PIVOT- C.C.W.	SLOW	For Road to Cal. Tom & Al in desert
10	PIVOT 90 TO FACE S.L.	PIVOT- C.C.W.	NORM	For Road to Cal. Casy & Uncle John
11	PIVOT 85 TO FACE U.S. (SLIGHT DIAG.)	PIVOT- C.C.W.	NORM	For Agricultural inspection

CUE #	MOVE (Pivots in Degrees)	DIRECTION	SPEED	SCENE
12	PIVOT 185 TO FACE D.S.	PIVOT- C.C.W.	NORM	At end inspection
13	DURING INTERMISSION PIVOT 90 TO FACE S.R.- STOP - THEN EXIT S.L. WING BACKING OFF	PIVOT-C.W. R. TO L.	NORM NORM	
14	ENTER FROM S.L. WING- GO FWD TO S.L.C. - STOP	L. TO R.	NORM	During Hooverville - getting ready to leave.
15	GO FWD & EXIT S.R. WING	L. TO R.	NORM	At end of Hooverville

APPENDIX H

FLY CUES

Note that the tab curtains were used to mask the truck in the wings, and to mask the wings in general. The rest of the flying pieces were as follows:

Uncle John's house — a flat wall with a screen door in it.
Gas Station sign
Star drop — star effect for night scenes
Backwall — a fullstage wooden wall with five doors in it, also
    rigged to split in half as "barn doors" in final scene
Weed Patch Camp sign — described in script
Gate — a chain link fence with barbed wire on top
Casy's tent — a square of canvas
Upstage Boxcar — a low full stage wooden wall
Downstage Boxcar — the outside of a boxcar, with a scrim
    panel on the Joad's half, opaque on the other side
Barn truss

FLY MOVEMENT

CUE #	MOVE	DIRECTION	SPEED	SCENE
1	TAB S.R.	OUT	FAST	IN CAR SALES. SONG
2	UNCLE JOHN'S HOUSE	IN	MED	IN CAR SALES. SONG
3	TAB S.R.	IN	MED	IN CAR SALES. SONG
4	UNCLE JOHN'S HOUSE	OUT	SLOW	END UNCLE JOHN SC.
5	TAB S.R.	OUT	MED	INTO PRO-PRIETOR SC.
6	TAB S.R.	IN	SLOW	TO MASK TRUCK
7	TAB S.R.– WHEN TRUCK CLEAR	OUT	MED	END PROPRIE-TOR SC.
	FOLLOW TAB S.R.	IN	MED	
8	GAS STATION SIGN	IN	MED	FOR GAS STATION
9	GAS STATION SIGN	OUT	MED	END GAS STATION
10	STAR DROP	IN	MED	FOR DESERT TOM/AL
11	STAR DROP	OUT	FAST	END AGRI. INSPECT.
INTERMISSION -				
	BACKWALL	IN	MED	
	TAB S.L.	OUT	SLOW	
12	TAB S.R. FOR FLOYD'S CAR	OUT+IN	MED	AS FLOYD EXITS
13	TAB S.L.	IN	MED	AFTER TRUCK ENTERS

CUE #	MOVE	DIRECTION	SPEED	SCENE
14	TAB S.R.	OUT	FAST	END HOOVER VILLE
15	BACKWALL	OUT	FAST	END HOOVER VILLE
	WEED PATCH SIGN	IN	FAST	
16	TAB S.R.	IN	MED	END HOOVER VILLE
17	WEEDPATCH SIGN	OUT	MED	END WEED PATCH
18	GATE	IN	MED	FOR HOOPER RANCH
19	GATE	OUT	MED	BOOKKEEPER EXITS
20	CASY'S TENT	IN	MED	FOR CASY'S TENT
	STAR DROP	IN	MED	SCENE
21	STAR DROP	OUT	MED	WITH B.O. FOR FIGHT
22	U.S. BOXCAR	IN	MED to SLOW	END OF FIGHT FOR MA & TOM SCENE
	CASY'S TENT	OUT	FAST	
23	D.S. BOXCAR	IN	MED	END MA & TOM SCENE
	BACKWALL	IN	FAST	
24	D.S. BOXCAR	OUT	MED	AS JOADS LEAVE
	U.S. BOXCAR	OUT	MED	BOXCARS
25	BARN TRUSS	IN	FAST	FOR BARN SCENE

APPENDIX I

The Grapes Of Wrath
SOUND CUES

Sound Cue List

Cue #	Effect	Scene
A	BIRD CALL	Tom & Casy Meet
B	DOG BARKS	Mulcy
C	CAR APPROACH	Muley
D	DOG BARKS	Muley
E	CAR PASSES	Proprietor
F	BIRDS SING	The Road to California
G	BIRDS SING	The Road to California
H	BIRDS SING	The Road to California
I	FIRE CRACKLING	End - Hooverville
I OUT	FIRE SOUND OUT	End - Hooverville
J	ONSTAGE MIKE UP	Weedpatch
J OUT	ONSTAGE MIKE OUT	Weedpatch
K	CRICKETS SOUND UP & CROWD NOISE UP	Hooper Ranch
K OUT	CROWD NOISE OUT (CRICKETS CONTINUE)	Hooper Ranch
L	DOG BARKS	Hooper Ranch
M	XF TO NEW CRICKETS SOUND	Casy's tent at the strike
M OUT	CRICKETS OUT	Top - Ma & Tom say goodbye
N	DOG BARKS	Ma & Tom say goodbye
O	DISTANT THUNDER	Boxcar

Cue #	Effect	Scene
P	ROLLING THUNDER TRACK & ADD RUMBLE TRACK	Boxcar
Q	THUNDER	Boxcar
R	THUNDER	Boxcar
S	THUNDER	Boxcar
T	THUNDER	Boxcar
U	BIG THUNDER	Boxcar
V	COTTONWOOD TREE FALLS	Boxcar
W	THUNDER	Boxcar
X	THUNDER	Boxcar
Y	THUNDER	Boxcar
Z	BIG THUNDER	Boxcar
AA	THUNDER	Boxcar
BB	THUNDER	Boxcar
CC	THUNDER	Boxcar
P OUT	ROLLING THUNDER TRACK & RUMBLE OUT	Top - Barn

NOTES:

1) The crowd noise cue was used to augment the shouting actors in the Hooper Ranch strike scene. It went out with the shotgun blast.

2) The rolling thunder track was a long tape of random thunder cues that played through the scene. The rumble track was just that, it was fed through sub-woofers to add a deep background sound.

3) The onstage mike was used in the square dance in the Weedpatch scene.

4) Although there are no listed cues for them, the members of the band wore wireless, microphones. This allowed the band to play in the wings and still be heard. They were also used to help fill out the sound when needed.

APPENDIX J

GRAMPA'S GRAVE

Grampa's grave is a just a trap in the floor filled with dirt. The inside sides of the trap should be constructed out of hard surfaced material, since the actors will use shovels to remove the dirt. When buying dirt for the trap, try to avoid potting soil that contains large amounts of styrofoam chips. In New York, the action of the scene was the actors shoveling the dirt out onto the top of the opened trap lid, then placing a dummy of Grampa into the trap, and then after the prayer, the actors shoveling the dirt back into the trap. The only problem encountered in this, was dirt building up on the edge that the trap lid sat on. In New York the lid was built in such a way that no lip or edge was needed to support the lid on the side that the actors put the dirt. The handles were recessed into the floor.

APPENDIX K

INFORMATION ABOUT MUSIC

NOTE ABOUT THE MUSIC USED IN
THE GRAPES OF WRATH

The inclusion of lyrics and the mention of song titles in the script of *The Grapes of Wrath* does not imply the granting of rights to use that material in other productions. Please contact the holder of the copyright.

"Yes, Sir, That's My Baby" written by Walter Donaldson and Gus Kahn, copyright owners Donaldson Publishing co. and Gilbert Keyes Music Co.

"California, Here I Come" by Joseph Meyer, Al Jolson, and Buddy DeSylva, copyright owner Warner Brothers, Inc.

For information regarding Michael Smith's original score for *The Grapes of Wrath*, please see the copyright page of this script.

APPENDIX L

SCENIC ELEMENTS

Following is a list of all the large (non-prop) set pieces in the show and the scenes that they play in.

The Grapes of Wrath
SET ELEMENTS TRACKING SHEET

PRESET
Truck set in S.R. wing facing S.L. wing
Truck masking in
All other flies out
River closed
Grave closed
Fire boxes closed
Fence set diagonally across stage

TOP OF SHOW
Turn smoke on & off

SONG - DUST BOWL FOLK SONG
Shift fence to second position
Set porch post S.R.

DURING MULEY
Turn center firebox on
Turn center firebox off

DURING "CAR SALESMAN SONG"
Strike fence from S.L. to S.R.
Strike porch post
Truck masking flies out
Truck enters from off S.R.; moves to onstage S.L. position
Uncle John's house flies in

DURING UNCLE JOHN'S HOUSE
Turn right firebox on
Turn right firebox off
Truck backs up to C.; pivots to face D.S.

DURING "66" SONG
Uncle John's house flies out
Truck pivots to face S.R.; moves S.R.
Turn center firebox on
Grave opens

DURING DUST BOWL HYMN
Turn center firebox off
Grave closes
Truck backs up to C.; pivots to face D.S.
Turn smoke on & off

TRANSITION FROM MA & AL IN TRUCK TO PROPRIETOR SCENE
Truck pivots to face S.R.; exits into S.R. wing
Turn center firebox on
Turn smoke on & off
Set tent city
Set porch post S.L.

TRANSITION FROM PROPRIETOR'S TO GAS STATION
Turn center firebox off
Strike tent city
Strike porch post
Truck backs onstage to C.; pivots to face D.S.
Gas sign flies in

TRANSITION FROM GAS STATION TO NARRATION AT THE RIVER
Gas sign flies out

DURING NARRATION AT RIVER
River opens
Truck pivots to face U.S. at a slight diagonal

TRANSITION FROM AT THE COLORADO RIVER TO THE ROAD TO CALIFORNIA
River closes
Truck pivots to face D.S. (Tom and Al scene)
Star drop flies in

DURING THE ROAD TO CALIFORNIA
Truck pivots to face S.L. (Casy and Uncle John scene)
Truck pivots to face U.S. at a slight diagonal (agricultural
    inspection)
Star drop flies out
Truck pivots to face D.S. (in California)

INTERMISSION
Truck pivots to face S.R.; back off into S.L. wing
Back wall flies in; its five doors are opened
Sweep and mop stage
Hang 3 clotheslines
Set Floyd's car in portal 2
Clean out fireboxes
Open right and left fireboxes

DURING HOOVERVILLE
Turn right and left fireboxes on
Strike clotheslines
Turn right firebox off
Turn left firebox off
Strike Floyd's car
Close doors on back wall (moving U.S. of the wall from S.L.
    to S.R.)
Truck enters from S.L. wing to onstage L.

TRANSITION FROM HOOVERVILLE TO
WEEDPATCH CAMP
Truck moves across stage and exits into S.R. wing
Truck masking flies in
Back wall flies out
Weedpatch sign flies in

DURING WEEDPATCH
Set microphone onstage

TRANSITION FROM WEEDPATCH TO
THE HOOPER RANCH
Strike microphone from onstage to S.L.
Weedpatch sign flies out
Gate flies in

DURING THE HOOPER RANCH
Gate flies out

DURING TRANSITION FROM HOOPER
RANCH TO CASY'S TENT
Casy's tent flies in
Star drop flies in

DURING CASY'S TENT
Turn left firebox on
Turn left firebox off
Star drop flies out

TRANSITION FROM CASY'S TENT TO MA
AND TOM SAY GOODBYE
Casy's tent flies out
U.S. Boxcar wall flies in

TRANSITION FROM MA AND TOM SAY
GOODBYE TO BOXCAR CAMP
River opens
D.S. Boxcar wall flies in
Back wall flies in

DURING BOXCAR CAMP
Turn rain (downpour) on
Turn rain (mist) on
Turn rain (downpour) off

TRANSITION FROM BOXCAR CAMP TO BARN
U.S. and D.S. Boxcar walls fly out
Barn truss flies in
Turn rain (mist) off
Open back wall for barn doors

TRANSITION FROM BARN TO CURTAIN CALL
River closes

WHITE CYC.

STAR DROP

BLACK SCRIM

HOOVERVILLE WALL (DOORS OPEN) AND BARN WALL (DOORS CLOSED)
N.B. BARNWALL SPLITS & SLIDES OPEN FOR BARN SCENE

UNCLE JOHN'S HOUSE

CASY'S TENT IN THE STRIKE — WEEDPATCH CAMP SIGN

+2'6" RAMP △

UPSTAGE BOXCAR WALL

HOOPER RANCH GATE — GRAMPA GRAVE TRAP

BARN TRUSS

DOWNSTAGE BOXCAR WALL N.B. S.L. OF ARCH IS SCRIM WALL

SLOT IN STAGE FLOOR FOR JOAD TRUCK MECHANISM

N.B. FLOOR SURFACE MUST BE SMOOTH ENOUGH FOR TRUCK TO SPIN ON.

FIRE PIT #2

FIRE PIT #1

FIRE PIT #3

GAS STATION SIGN

+1'6" RAMP △ +0'6"

PROS.

RIVER TRAP (RAIN PIPES ABOVE)

5TH PORTAL
4TH PORTAL
3RD PORTAL
2ND PORTAL
1ST PORTAL

SCENE DESIGN

"THE GRAPES OF WRATH"

NEW PLAYS

★ **MONTHS ON END by Craig Pospisil.** In comic scenes, one for each month of the year, we follow the intertwined worlds of a circle of friends and family whose lives are poised between happiness and heartbreak. "...a triumph...these twelve vignettes all form crucial pieces in the eternal puzzle known as human relationships, an area in which the playwright displays an assured knowledge that spans deep sorrow to unbounded happiness." –*Ann Arbor News.* "...rings with emotional truth, humor...[an] endearing contemplation on love...entertaining and satisfying." –*Oakland Press.* [5M, 5W] ISBN: 0-8222-1892-5

★ **GOOD THING by Jessica Goldberg.** Brings us into the households of John and Nancy Roy, forty-something high-school guidance counselors whose marriage has been increasingly on the rocks and Dean and Mary, recent graduates struggling to make their way in life. "...a blend of gritty social drama, poetic humor and unsubtle existential contemplation..." –*Variety.* [3M, 3W] ISBN: 0-8222-1869-0

★ **THE DEAD EYE BOY by Angus MacLachlan.** Having fallen in love at their Narcotics Anonymous meeting, Billy and Shirley-Diane are striving to overcome the past together. But their relationship is complicated by the presence of Sorin, Shirley-Diane's fourteen-year-old son, a damaged reminder of her dark past. "...a grim, insightful portrait of an unmoored family..." –*NY Times.* "MacLachlan's play isn't for the squeamish, but then, tragic stories delivered at such an unrelenting fever pitch rarely are." –*Variety.* [1M, 1W, 1 boy] ISBN: 0-8222-1844-5

★ **[SIC] by Melissa James Gibson.** In adjacent apartments three young, ambitious neighbors come together to discuss, flirt, argue, share their dreams and plan their futures with unequal degrees of deep hopefulness and abject despair. "A work...concerned with the sound and power of language..." –*NY Times.* "...a wonderfully original take on urban friendship and the comedy of manners—a *Design for Living* for our times..." –*NY Observer.* [3M, 2W] ISBN: 0-8222-1872-0

★ **LOOKING FOR NORMAL by Jane Anderson.** Roy and Irma's twenty-five-year marriage is thrown into turmoil when Roy confesses that he is actually a woman trapped in a man's body, forcing the couple to wrestle with the meaning of their marriage and the delicate dynamics of family. "Jane Anderson's bittersweet transgender domestic comedy-drama ...is thoughtful and touching and full of wit and wisdom. A real audience pleaser." –*Hollywood Reporter.* [5M, 4W] ISBN: 0-8222-1857-7

★ **ENDPAPERS by Thomas McCormack.** The regal Joshua Maynard, the old and ailing head of a mid-sized, family-owned book-publishing house in New York City, must name a successor. One faction in the house backs a smart, "pragmatic" manager, the other faction a smart, "sensitive" editor and both factions fear what the other's man could do to this house— and to them. "If Kaufman and Hart had undertaken a comedy about the publishing business, they might have written *Endpapers*...a breathlessly fast, funny, and thoughtful comedy ...keeps you amused, guessing, and often surprised...profound in its empathy for the paradoxes of human nature." –*NY Magazine.* [7M, 4W] ISBN: 0-8222-1908-5

★ **THE PAVILION by Craig Wright.** By turns poetic and comic, romantic and philosophical, this play asks old lovers to face the consequences of difficult choices made long ago. "The script's greatest strength lies in the genuineness of its feeling." –*Houston Chronicle.* "Wright's perceptive, gently witty writing makes this familiar situation fresh and thoroughly involving." –*Philadelphia Inquirer.* [2M, 1W (flexible casting)] ISBN: 0-8222-1898-4

DRAMATISTS PLAY SERVICE, INC.
440 Park Avenue South, New York, NY 10016 212-683-8960 Fax 212-213-1539
postmaster@dramatists.com www.dramatists.com

NEW PLAYS

★ **BE AGGRESSIVE by Annie Weisman.** Vista Del Sol is paradise, sandy beaches, avocado-lined streets. But for seventeen-year-old cheerleader Laura, everything changes when her mother is killed in a car crash, and she embarks on a journey to the Spirit Institute of the South where she can learn "cheer" with Bible belt intensity. "...filled with lingual gymnastics...stylized rapid-fire dialogue..." *–Variety*. "...a new, exciting, and unique voice in the American theatre..." *–BackStage West*. [1M, 4W, extras] ISBN: 0-8222 1894-1

★ **FOUR by Christopher Shinn.** Four people struggle desperately to connect in this quiet, sophisticated, moving drama. "...smart, broken-hearted...Mr. Shinn has a precocious and forgiving sense of how power shifts in the game of sexual pursuit...He promises to be a playwright to reckon with..." *–NY Times*. "A voice emerges from an American place. It's got humor, sadness and a fresh and touching rhythm that tell of the loneliness and secrets of life...[a] poetic, haunting play." *–NY Post*. [3M, 1W] ISBN: 0-8222-1850-X

★ **WONDER OF THE WORLD by David Lindsay-Abaire.** A madcap picaresque involving Niagara Falls, a lonely tour-boat captain, a pair of bickering private detectives and a husband's dirty little secret. "Exceedingly whimsical and playfully wicked. Winning and genial. A top-drawer production." *–NY Times*. "Full frontal lunacy is on display. A most assuredly fresh and hilarious tragicomedy of marital discord run amok...absolutely hysterical..." *–Variety*. [3M, 4W (doubling)] ISBN: 0-8222-1863-1

★ **QED by Peter Parnell.** Nobel Prize winning physicist and all-around genius Richard Feynman holds forth with captivating wit and wisdom in this fascinating biographical play that originally starred Alan Alda. "QED is a seductive mix of science, human affections, moral courage, and comic eccentricity. It reflects on, among other things, death, the absence of God, travel to an unexplored country, the pleasures of drumming, and the need to know and understand." *–NY Magazine*. "Its rhythms correspond to the way that people—even geniuses—approach and avoid highly emotional issues, and it portrays Feynman with affection and awe." *–The New Yorker*. [1M, 1W] ISBN: 0-8222-1924-7

★ **UNWRAP YOUR CANDY by Doug Wright.** Alternately chilling and hilarious, this deliciously macabre collection of four bedtime tales for adults is guaranteed to keep you awake for nights on end. "Engaging and intellectually satisfying...a treat to watch." *–NY Times*. "Fiendishly clever. Mordantly funny and chilling. Doug Wright teases, freezes and zaps us." *–Village Voice*. "Four bite-size plays that bite back." *–Variety*. [flexible casting] ISBN: 0-8222-1871-2

★ **FURTHER THAN THE FURTHEST THING by Zinnie Harris.** On a remote island in the middle of the Atlantic secrets are buried. When the outside world comes calling, the islanders find their world blown apart from the inside as well as beyond. "Harris winningly produces an intimate and poetic, as well as political, family saga." *–Independent (London)*. "Harris' enthralling adventure of a play marks a departure from stale, well-furrowed theatrical terrain." *–Evening Standard (London)*. [3M, 2W] ISBN: 0-8222-1874-7

★ **THE DESIGNATED MOURNER by Wallace Shawn.** The story of three people living in a country where what sort of books people like to read and how they choose to amuse themselves becomes both firmly personal and unexpectedly entangled with questions of survival. "This is a playwright who does not just tell you what it is like to be arrested at night by goons or to fall morally apart and become an aimless yet weirdly contented ghost yourself. He has the originality to make you feel it." *–Times (London)*. "A fascinating play with beautiful passages of writing..." *–Variety*. [2M, 1W] ISBN: 0-8222-1848-8

DRAMATISTS PLAY SERVICE, INC.
440 Park Avenue South, New York, NY 10016 212-683-8960 Fax 212-213-1539
postmaster@dramatists.com   www.dramatists.com

NEW PLAYS

★ **SHEL'S SHORTS by Shel Silverstein.** Lauded poet, songwriter and author of children's books, the incomparable Shel Silverstein's short plays are deeply infused with the same wicked sense of humor that made him famous. "…[a] childlike honesty and twisted sense of humor." —*Boston Herald.* "…terse dialogue and an absurdity laced with a tang of dread give [*Shel's Shorts*] more than a trace of Samuel Beckett's comic existentialism." —*Boston Phoenix.* [flexible casting] ISBN: 0-8222-1897-6

★ **AN ADULT EVENING OF SHEL SILVERSTEIN by Shel Silverstein.** Welcome to the darkly comic world of Shel Silverstein, a world where nothing is as it seems and where the most innocent conversation can turn menacing in an instant. These ten imaginative plays vary widely in content, but the style is unmistakable. "…[*An Adult Evening*] shows off Silverstein's virtuosic gift for wordplay…[and] sends the audience out…with a clear appreciation of human nature as perverse and laughable." —*NY Times.* [flexible casting] ISBN: 0-8222-1873-9

★ **WHERE'S MY MONEY? by John Patrick Shanley.** A caustic and sardonic vivisection of the institution of marriage, laced with the author's inimitable razor-sharp wit. "…Shanley's gift for acid-laced one-liners and emotionally tumescent exchanges is certainly potent…" —*Variety.* "…lively, smart, occasionally scary and rich in reverse wisdom." —*NY Times.* [3M, 3W] ISBN: 0-8222-1865-8

★ **A FEW STOUT INDIVIDUALS by John Guare.** A wonderfully screwy comedy-drama that figures Ulysses S. Grant in the throes of writing his memoirs, surrounded by a cast of fantastical characters, including the Emperor and Empress of Japan, the opera star Adelina Patti and Mark Twain. "Guare's smarts, passion and creativity skyrocket to awesome heights…" —*Star Ledger.* "…precisely the kind of good new play that you might call an everyday miracle…every minute of it is fresh and newly alive…" —*Village Voice.* [10M, 3W] ISBN: 0-8222-1907-7

★ **BREATH, BOOM by Kia Corthron.** A look at fourteen years in the life of Prix, a Bronx native, from her ruthless girl-gang leadership at sixteen through her coming to maturity at thirty. "…vivid world, believable and eye-opening, a place worthy of a dramatic visit, where no one would want to live but many have to." —*NY Times.* "…rich with humor, terse vernacular strength and gritty detail…" —*Variety.* [1M, 9W] ISBN: 0-8222-1849-6

★ **THE LATE HENRY MOSS by Sam Shepard.** Two antagonistic brothers, Ray and Earl, are brought together after their father, Henry Moss, is found dead in his seedy New Mexico home in this classic Shepard tale. "…His singular gift has been for building mysteries out of the ordinary ingredients of American family life…" —*NY Times.* "…rich moments …Shepard finds gold." —*LA Times.* [7M, 1W] ISBN: 0-8222-1858-5

★ **THE CARPETBAGGER'S CHILDREN by Horton Foote.** One family's history spanning from the Civil War to WWII is recounted by three sisters in evocative, intertwining monologues. "…bittersweet music—[a] rhapsody of ambivalence…in its modest, garrulous way…theatrically daring." —*The New Yorker.* [3W] ISBN: 0-8222-1843-7

★ **THE NINA VARIATIONS by Steven Dietz.** In this funny, fierce and heartbreaking homage to *The Seagull*, Dietz puts Chekhov's star-crossed lovers in a room and doesn't let them out. "A perfect little jewel of a play…" —*Shepherdstown Chronicle.* "…a delightful revelation of a writer at play; and also an odd, haunting, moving theater piece of lingering beauty." —*Eastside Journal (Seattle).* [1M, 1W (flexible casting)] ISBN: 0-8222-1891-7

DRAMATISTS PLAY SERVICE, INC.
440 Park Avenue South, New York, NY 10016 212-683-8960 Fax 212-213-1539
postmaster@dramatists.com www.dramatists.com